THROUGH CANADA
WITH A KODAK

THROUGH CANADA
WITH A KODAK

THE COUNTESS OF
ABERDEEN

Introduction by
Marjory Harper

UNIVERSITY OF TORONTO PRESS
Toronto Buffalo London

© University of Toronto Press Incorporated 1994
Toronto Buffalo London
Printed in Canada
ISBN 0-8020-7765-x (paper)

∞

Printed on acid-free paper

Canadian Cataloguing in Publication Data

Aberdeen and Temair, Ishbel Gordon, Marchioness
of, 1857–1939
Through Canada with a Kodak

Includes index.
ISBN 0-8020-7765-x

1. Aberdeen and Temair, Ishbel Gordon, Marchioness of, 1857–1939 – Journeys – Canada.   2. Canada – Description and travel.   3. Canada – History – 1867–1914.   I. Harper, Marjory.   II. Title.

FC73.A24 1994   917.104′54   C94-930893-5
F1015.A24 1994

This book has been published with the help of grants from The Carnegie Trust for the Universities of Scotland; the Department of History and Economic History, the Faculty of Arts and Divinity, the University Studies Committee, and the Centre for Scottish Studies, all of the University of Aberdeen; the University of Aberdeen Development Trust; and the Scouloudi Foundation Historical Awards.

MAY I commend Dr Marjory Harper's *Through Canada with a Kodak*. My great predecessor, Ishbel, Lady Aberdeen, was a tremendous lady in so many fields, and was particularly active in women's organizations, but she was also splendid with a camera and her historical sense was wonderfully descriptive. She loved Canada and took an immense interest in its beauty and its history and the book is a wonderful record of those early days when she first went there.

I congratulate Dr Harper on her research and on this interesting Manuscript.

June, Marchioness of Aberdeen & Temair.
Haddo House
Aberdeen

CONTENTS

Acknowledgments	ix
Introduction to the 1994 Edition	xiii
Notes	lxxvi
Through Canada with a Kodak	lxxxvii
Annotated List of Illustrations	251
Index	275

ACKNOWLEDGMENTS

THIS publication would not have been possible without considerable financial assistance. I wish to acknowledge external grants from two trusts, The Scouloudi Foundation, in association with the Institute of Historical Research, and the Carnegie Trust for the Universities of Scotland. Further support was provided by the University of Aberdeen, through grants from the University Studies Committee, the Faculty of Arts and Divinity, and the Centre for Scottish Studies, as well as through a grant and loan from the Department of History. I am particularly grateful to Professor Roy Bridges for his help in securing such funding.

Permission to make use of unpublished papers in the Haddo House Archive and to reproduce photographs from the private albums of the Aberdeen family was granted by the Earl of Haddo. I am most grateful to Lady Aberdeen for writing a foreword to this new edition of her predecessor's travel writings, and to the staff of the National Trust for Scotland for giving me ready

Acknowledgments

access to the library and muniment room at Haddo House. Andrew Rodger, Photo-Archivist in the Documentary Art and Photography Division, National Archives of Canada, gave generously of his time and expertise in identifying many of the photographs, and Wayne Norton of Kamloops, British Columbia, shared the fruits of his research into the Killarney and Saltcoats settlements.

I am particularly grateful to Donald Paterson and Norman Little, both of Aberdeen University, for preparing many of the original photographs for republication, and to the Aberdeen University Department of Geography for providing the essential new ingredient of a map. Aberdeen University Library generously gave permission for its copy of the original publication to be sent to Canada for rephotographing.

*Opposite: The Dominion of Canada,
showing the route taken by Lady Aberdeen in 1890*

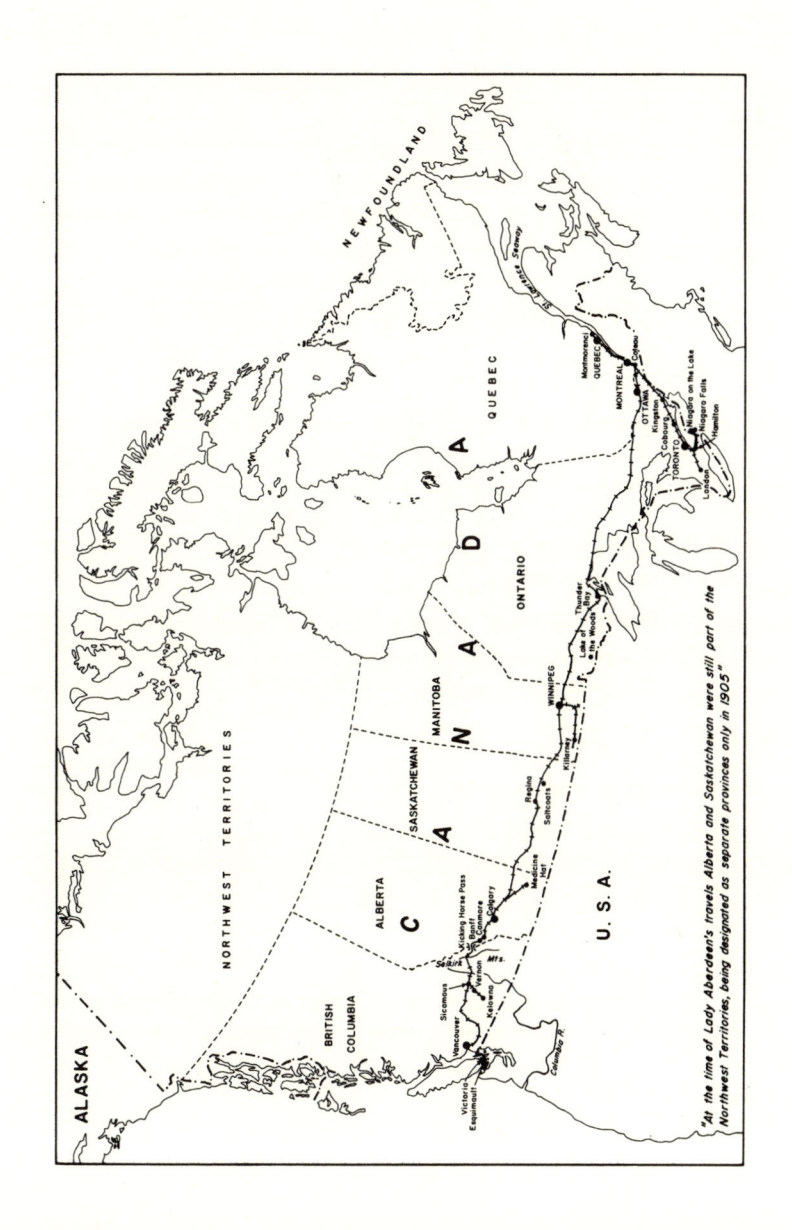

"At the time of Lady Aberdeen's travels Alberta and Saskatchewan were still part of the Northwest Territories, being designated as separate provinces only in 1905."

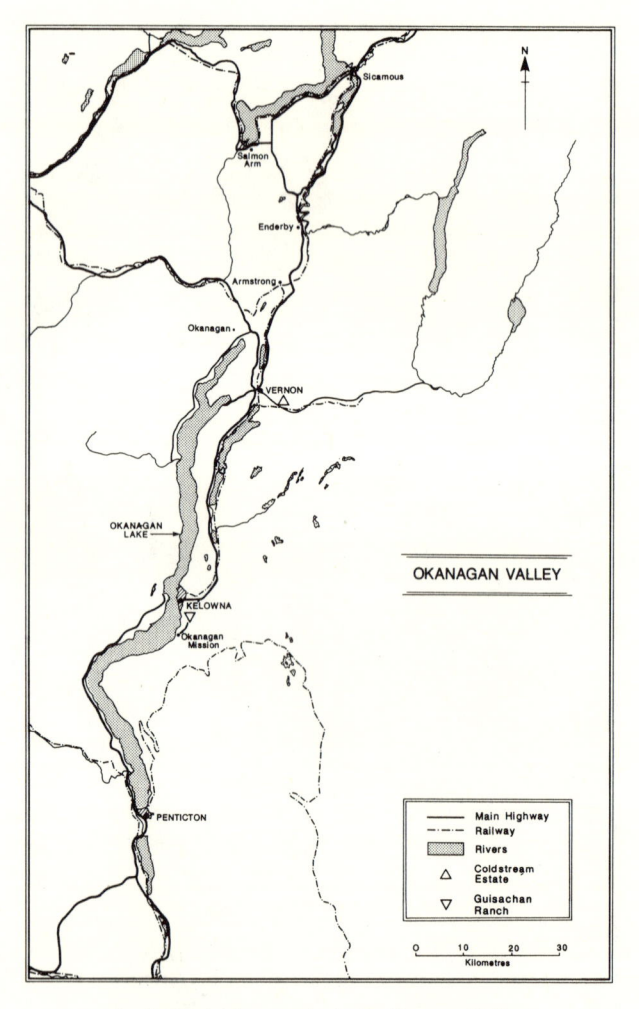

Lady Aberdeen's properties in the Okanagan Valley

INTRODUCTION TO THE 1994 EDITION

Transatlantic Travelogues

Throughout the nineteenth century the British reading public was regularly bombarded with descriptive and promotional literature on Britain's expanding colonial possessions. As both emigration and tourism expanded, casual visitors and serious settlers alike were confronted by a bewildering array of travelogues and emigrant guidebooks offering information and advice on a wide variety of destinations. Canada always featured prominently in this flood of publications, notably in the second half of the century, when the Dominion government, worried by American competition, launched a concerted campaign to attract settlers, particularly to its vast western territories. This campaign reached its climax at the turn of the century, as the Laurier administration committed ever more resources to both printed propaganda and personal agency activity in Britain, Europe, and the United States, a commitment which saw the federal immigration budget escalate from $400,000 in 1896 to $4,000,000 in 1906.[1]

But the promotion of Canada in Britain was not the exclusive preserve of the federal government. The provincial authorities, transcontinental railway companies, land developers, and a host of amateur agents also bent the ears of the British public with lectures, exhibitions, press advertisements, articles, pamphlets, and handbooks of varying size, sophistication, and usefulness. Not all the literature pertaining to Canada was intended to promote immigration, but even disinterested commentators – dilettante travellers and armchair observers, for example – played their part in popularizing the Dominion among a British readership inspired by the concept of a new Age of Imperialism and fascinated by the romantic image of the North American frontier. Indeed, throughout the nineteenth century the steady evolution of a tourist industry in North America owed much to the influence of romanticism, with its elevation of the aesthetic virtues of the untamed wilderness and its eulogizing of chivalric heroes who personified the spirit of the nation. Uncleared bush, raging cataracts, unbroken prairie, and forbidding mountain ranges embodied the essential motifs of the primitive and the sublime so cherished by the romantics, and the image of the unspoiled frontier – retreating ever westwards as settlement advanced – was promoted unceasingly in travel narratives, guidebooks, novels, and poetry, alongside the heroic exploits of the conquering pioneers who had shaped the nation's identity.[2]

Introduction to the 1994 Edition

It was in this climate of national enthusiasm for the Dominion among the British reading, travelling, and emigrating public that *Through Canada with a Kodak* was published in Edinburgh in 1893. Like many contemporary publications, it took the form of a journal, recording two trips made by the author to Canada, one in 1890 and one in 1891. Having first appeared as a serial in Lady Aberdeen's estate magazine, *Onward and Upward*, it was subsequently made available in book form by W.H. White & Co., the Edinburgh printers, process engravers, publishers, and booksellers, apparently in response to public demand. The first issue to go on sale (in September 1893) was a paperback, retailing at two shillings through the wholesale booksellers Simpkin Marshall of London. A hardback version followed hard on its heels, 'published at 3s. 6d., with gold stamped sides and gilt top.'[3] In 1896 W.H. White & Co., by then a limited company operating under the new name of Riverside Press and specializing in sporting, literary, and travel material, published a second edition of *Through Canada with a Kodak*, in both paperback and hardback. By 1899 a popular edition in quarto format was retailing at only sixpence.

In the absence of specific records or statements by the publisher it is impossible to determine the total number of copies printed. However, the print run was probably very large, perhaps running into tens of thousands, since it would hardly have paid the publisher to produce a limited print run of a book originally retailing at two shillings in paperback. But Lady Aberdeen's illustrated travel journal evidently caught and held the public imagination, justifying the high-profile advertisements taken out by the publishers in the Edinburgh Post Office Directory in the mid-1890s. A book which generated a hardback edition, a second edition in both paperback and hardback, and a popular edition in only seven years clearly belied its author's professed belief that her writings were 'scarcely worthy of being thus collected in the form of a volume.' Nor were they, as she claimed, 'merely the passing and superficial notes of a traveller journeying rapidly through the country' and 'the recollections of delightful holiday trips.' This book cannot be classified simply as a disinterested travelogue, for Lady Aberdeen aimed to influence as well as inform. Since she was an enthusiastic Canadianist, her writings reinforced the positive image of Canada cultivated by the professional propagandists, while at the same time demonstrating the extent to which her own perceptions had been affected by earlier image makers.

The Countess of Aberdeen

Lady Aberdeen's interest in Canada developed initially out of her support for the subsidized emigration of working-class women, and predated her first visit to the Dominion by some seven years. Throughout her long life she was an ardent crusader for women's welfare and advancement, at all levels of society and on both sides of the Atlantic. Domestic and political influences in her childhood undoubtedly helped to shape her subsequent feminism. Ishbel Maria Marjoribanks was born in London in 1857, into a well-connected family which derived its wealth from brewing and banking enterprises. The third of five surviving children, the perceptive Ishbel soon became aware of her parents' unhappy marital relations, manifested, it seems, in her father's violent and tyrannical treatment of her mother, which was reciprocated by his wife's careful cultivation of a martyr complex.[4] Ishbel's childhood reaction was to rebel against parental authority and to become increasingly alienated from her father; in adulthood she channelled her energies and leadership abilities into campaigning for women's occupational, political, and social rights at home and abroad. In Britain she advocated the admission of women to the ministry and, as President of the Women's Liberal Federation, she championed the cause of female suffrage. In Ireland she created a pioneering mother-and-child welfare organization, the Women's National Health Association of Ireland, and also launched a successful crusade against tuberculosis. While resident in Canada she helped to initiate the creation of a Dominion-wide health service through her foundation of the Victorian Order of Nurses in 1897 in commemoration of Queen Victoria's Diamond Jubilee. In an international sphere, she was from 1893 to 1936 President of the International Council of Women, a body created in 1888 to promote the social, economic, and political welfare of women.

Politics supplied the other major formative influence on Ishbel's youth and remained a passionate interest for the rest of her life. Her father, Edward Marjoribanks (in 1881 elevated to the peerage as Baron Tweedmouth), was a Liberal member of Parliament, and his daughter grew up in a household where William Ewart Gladstone, Liberal leader and four-times prime minister, was a frequent and welcome visitor. Persistent efforts by Ishbel and her mother eventually won her, at the age of twenty, the hand of John Gordon, the diffident seventh Earl of Aberdeen, whose inherited Conservatism was soon – if somewhat painfully – replaced by commitment to Gladstonian Liberalism at the insistence of his determined young wife.[5] On her marriage in 1877 Ishbel's political activities were transferred to her husband's estate at Haddo in northeast Scotland, which she rapidly turned into a noted hotbed of Liberalism, through political dinner-parties at which Gladstone, Lord Rosebery, and other leading Liberals were the honoured guests.

But Ishbel brought more than a new political focus to

Aberdeenshire. From the outset she demonstrated a wide-ranging, if sometimes dictatorial, Christian concern for social welfare within and beyond northeast Scotland, developing and sustaining her involvement through an intricate network of prominent evangelical contacts. Gladstone's influence had inspired her with charitable zeal as well as lifelong Liberalism, a trait which she had demonstrated even in her teens, when she became involved with rescue work among London prostitutes. During their honeymoon on the Nile, she and Lord Aberdeen adopted four Arab slave children, whom they enrolled in an Presbyterian mission school at Asyut, after renaming them Campbell, Aberdeen, Gordon, and Haddo.[6] Once installed at Haddo House, Ishbel's initial concern was for her own household servants and estate tenants. This attitude was in keeping with the Aberdeens' traditionally benevolent estate policy, which a generation earlier had seen the erection of workers' cottages at a time when many other landlords were demolishing such dwellings and evicting their occupants, and which in the seventh Earl's time saw regular rent remissions to compensate tenants for bad harvests and depressed agricultural conditions.[7]

Among Ishbel's early contributions to this benevolent estate policy were the establishment of a cottage hospital and district nurse at the village of Tarves and the opening (by Gladstone) of a female orphanage in the village of Methlick.[8] For her own household servants she organized Bible study, needlework, and history classes, before turning her attention to domestic servants elsewhere on the estate, encouraging them to continue and broaden their education through evening classes and distance learning. As a result the Haddo House Association was born in December 1881, when Ishbel enlisted the help of several of her tenant farmers' wives to teach and supervise the correspondence courses which she herself compiled. Within a year the Association had enrolled over eight hundred girls and five hundred mistresses, and the first of Ishbel's many publications, in 1884, was a homily on the best means of promoting mutual understanding and loyalty between mistresses and servants.[9]

By 1891 the Haddo House Association had become so well-known, with over one hundred branches at home and abroad, that its name was changed to the less parochial Onward and Upward Association.[10] From 1891 to 1930 its mouthpiece, the *Onward and Upward* magazine, was distributed monthly to members all over the world, Lady Aberdeen having enlisted the help of the eminent London journalist W.T. Stead in securing cheap production facilities in the capital and free transportation to hundreds of emigrant associates. This journal, which contained a miscellany of fictional and non-fictional articles, a children's section, quizzes, practical hints, and spiritual encouragement, provided the initial forum for

Introduction to the 1994 Edition   xxi

the publication of *Through Canada with a Kodak*, which appeared in lavishly illustrated monthly instalments in 1891 and 1892.

By that time Lady Aberdeen's concern for the welfare of working-class women had already brought her into regular contact with Canada and Canadians. In November 1883, concerned about the social, economic, and moral prospects of factory girls, shop assistants, and fishwives in the city of Aberdeen, she founded the Aberdeen Ladies' Union in order to coordinate the many different branches of female welfare work already operating in that city. Within a month over two hundred like-minded women joined her organization, and substantial donations allowed the Ladies' Union to run evening educational and recreational clubs for working girls, as well as to establish an employment registry, servants' training home, and lodging house. Integral to the whole operation was the promotion of subsidized emigration, for the Countess of Aberdeen, like many of her fellow-philanthropists, was firmly convinced of the value of emigration as a means of assisting not only the emigrants themselves, but also the society which they left and the countries where they settled. The training home offered instruction in colonial as well as domestic skills, the employment registry advertised overseas as well as domestic situations, and between 1884 and 1913 a special committee of the Ladies' Union assisted or supervised the emigration of 379 girls from Aberdeen and northeast Scotland, at least 296 of them to Canada.[11]

The Aberdeens' first trip to Canada, in 1890, was in fact provoked partly by Ishbel's desire to check up on former recruits and to investigate personally the case for the emigration of selected individuals and groups as a solution to socio-economic problems in Britain. Although this was perhaps not the ideal rest cure for the nervous breakdown she had suffered the previous year, it did at least remove her temporarily from the cauldron of Liberal politics at home, where, in 1886, the defeat of her friend and mentor Gladstone on the issue of Irish Home Rule had precipitated an irrevocable split in the party. The keen support for well-conducted emigration Ishbel demonstrated on this trip is reflected in the frequent anecdotes regarding settlers and settlement recorded in *Through Canada with a Kodak*, and in the fact that eight of the household servants who accompanied the family were to remain permanently in Canada, with their employers' blessing.[12] Lady Aberdeen's interest in all aspects of Canadian life was reinforced by subsequent visits to the Dominion, particularly by the family's five-year residence there from 1893 to 1898, when her husband served as governor general. During this period her impressions of Canadian politics, society, and culture were faithfully and frequently committed to her journal and subsequently recalled in several of her later publications.[13]

Although 1890 saw the Aberdeens' first trip to Canada, they were already seasoned world travellers. Their honeymoon in 1877 had taken them to Egypt, Italy, and Paris, and in 1887 they had undertaken a marathon tour of India, Australia, New Zealand, and the United States, where Lady Aberdeen's brothers Archie and Coutts were then managing cattle ranches in Texas and Dakota respectively on behalf of their father. But although these trips were recorded in her private diary and subsequently described in her memoirs, it was only after visiting Canada that Lady Aberdeen decided, in 1891, to write a contemporary travelogue for public consumption – her first and only venture into this writing genre.

The Photographs

In its structure and content, *Through Canada with a Kodak* conformed to the pattern of numerous amateur travelogues about the Dominion circulating in late nineteenth-century Britain, blending personal and family anecdotes, political opinions, and social commentary in the form of an edited journal. Its uniqueness lay in the quality and quantity of the illustrations which accompanied the text and made use of revolutionary advances in amateur photography pioneered in the United States in the 1880s.

For more than three decades successive technological

developments had been bringing the potential of photography increasingly within the reach of the interested amateur. Queen Victoria and her Consort were enthusiastic advocates of the new art form, and the Great Exhibition of 1851, masterminded by Prince Albert, demonstrated the most recent advances, particularly in France and the United States. A year later the first British photographic society was formed in London, and as the industry continued to be stimulated by royal encouragement and public demand for photographic portraits, so studios of varying standards sprang up all over the country, and a new vocabulary of photographic terms entered the language. By the 1890s mass-produced, hand-held stereoscopic viewers had become a standard feature of the middle-class Victorian parlour, bringing three-dimensional images of exotic lands and everyday scenes to home audiences. Similar professionally photographed travel views were displayed to public audiences through the device of lantern slides, and for several decades the 'lantern lecture' was used extensively by emigration and travel agents to enhance their numerous talks and exhibitions.

Yet the actual technique of photography remained an expensive, skilled, and time-consuming occupation, involving cumbersome and fragile equipment which was difficult to manipulate. Even the British discovery in 1851 of the wet collodion process (which reduced exposure time and used glass plates to produce a drastically improved image) and the French technique of multiple *carte de visite* portraits (small prints, mounted on card) did not inaugurate the age of the amateur photographer. That had to await the invention of dry plate negatives (resulting in even shorter exposures), roll films (which made cameras more portable), and processing laboratories (which undertook the complex and messy developing and printing functions). The real birth of instant snapshot photography came in the late 1880s with the development of a portable, hand-held camera, free of inhibiting tripod and complete with rollfilm holder, thus integrating camera, film, and – crucially – processing in one compact box. It was the brainchild of George Eastman, a bank clerk turned photographic manufacturer from Rochester, New York. He patented his first model in 1888, but a year later designed a much cheaper, simplified shutter for this camera, which he named the 'Kodak.' He also recognized that many interested amateurs did not have the time, inclination, or darkroom facilities to develop and print their own pictures, and so he established factories at Rochester and Harrow (England), where customers sent their film for unloading, processing, and printing. The camera was then reloaded with another 100-exposure spool and within ten days was returned to the customer, who could now enjoy the art of photography without worrying about the technicalities of making a print.[14]

In this way Eastman opened up a new world of snapshot photography to the enthusiastic but untrained amateur who could afford the twenty-five dollars (five guineas) required for the camera and ten dollars (two guineas) for the developing and printing. All that was required of the photographer was to set the shutter by pulling a string, aim the camera using V-lines embedded in the top of the box, press the release button, and wind on the film by turning a key. The new invention was an immediate success. By September 1889 over five thousand Kodaks had been sold in the United States, and an exhibition of amateur Kodak photographs held by the Eastman Company in London in 1897 attracted over twenty-five thousand entries.[15] Similar interest was shown in Canada, where amateur camera clubs mushroomed in the 1880s and 1890s, provoking the comment in 1898 from one Winnipeg enthusiast that 'from Cape Breton to the Pacific the kodak is abroad in the land.'[16]

Some credit for this should perhaps go the Countess of Aberdeen, who was one of the Kodak's earliest and most committed advocates. Attracted by Eastman's marketing slogan – 'You Press the Button – We Do the Rest' – she summoned an advertising agent to the family's London residence to demonstrate the simplicity and quality of 'a camera like a black shoe-box and spools of film with one hundred exposures.'[17] Completely won over, she made the purchase, and soon afterwards paid her first visit to Canada, during which the Kodak was her constant companion. Indeed, her published account of that trip itself helped further to popularize amateur photography in general and Eastman's invention in particular. Sixty years later her daughter recalled, 'There were many who first discovered the meaning of the new word Kodak from the breezy travel letters which she sent home for her magazine with her own snapshots as illustrations and her own "snappy" phrase as title: *Through Canada with a Kodak.*'[18]

The book contains a total of 120 illustrations – 84 photographs (including one repeat), 35 sketches, and a map. Eighteen of the sketches, all of Native artifacts, are attributed to one J. Grant, the remainder probably being the work of Lady Aberdeen herself, although only seven are ascribed specifically to her. Most of these sketches seem to have been based on professional photographs which Lady Aberdeen either purchased or was given during her Canadian trip. The Hamilton yacht sketch, for instance (page 51), is a direct copy of a photograph which appears in one of the Canadian albums at Haddo House under the caption 'White Wing – Champion Yacht,' and is probably the work of a professional photographer in Hamilton. The sketch of the University Buildings, Toronto (page 63), is based on a picture taken about 1870 by an unknown photographer, the original of which is located in the holdings of the National Archives of Canada. The sketches of the Darough homestead at Killarney (page 111), the Three Sisters mountain range (page 133), and Mount Rundle at Banff (page 136 – erroneously captioned as Cascade Mountain) are also based on photographs found in the family albums at Haddo House, while the illustrations of Native activities (pages 219 and 221) are modelled on photographs attributed to the Calgary firm of Boorne and May. The two other unattributed drawings – of the Aberdeens' railway-car attendant (page 95) and a prairie work gang (page 122) – could not be identified from photographs, although the former may have been based on a *carte de visite*.[19]

The eighty-four photographs were collected from a variety of sources. Forty-two were probably amateur Kodak snaps taken by Lady Aberdeen herself. In thirty-five cases, identical, or almost identical, prints have been located in three family albums at Haddo House, all but one of these being contained in two volumes devoted exclusively to the Aberdeens' early Canadian excursions.[20] Since Ishbel was not an expert photographer, several of these amateur snaps were considerably enhanced in the printing of *Through Canada with a Kodak*, to disguise defects evident in the original images. In fact, slight disparities between some of the published and unpublished Kodak pictures indicate that the images in the albums were simply duplicates – often inferior duplicates – of snaps which Ishbel submitted to

Introduction to the 1994 Edition xxix

the publisher and which were not subsequently returned to her.[21] The remaining forty-two photographs were generally of a much higher quality and were probably the work of a variety of professional photographers in both Canada and Britain. Copies of eighteen professional photographs which appear in *Through Canada with a Kodak* also appear in the family albums, and it is likely that many of them were gifts or purchases acquired during the Aberdeens' Canadian travels. Unfortunately, the quality of the photographs has deteriorated with the passage of a century, and the combined effects of careless mounting, poor storage, and the ravages of time are evident in the fading, cracking, and staining which it has been impossible to eradicate from the reproductions of several illustrations, both amateur and professional, used in this edition.

While some of the professional photographs are unattributed, special acknowledgment is made in *Through Canada with a Kodak* of the work of Messrs Notman of Montreal, and Messrs Boorne and May of Calgary. Both these firms were established by immigrants from Britain. William Notman (1826–91), who became Montreal's leading photographer in the late nineteenth century, was a native of Paisley in Scotland, where he had dabbled as an amateur in early photographic techniques. In 1856 he came to Canada, and by the end of the year he had established a successful photographic business in Montreal. All his three sons followed him into the business, and several more distant family members were also employed in his studios. One of his protégés was William James Topley, who in the 1890s was to take many official photographs of the Aberdeens during Lord Aberdeen's term of office as governor general. William Hanson Boorne was less well-known than Notman. He was an English chemist and enthusiastic amateur photographer who had settled as a homesteader in Manitoba in 1882. After moving to Calgary in 1885 he persuaded his cousin, Ernest May, to come out from England, and from 1886 to 1893 the two men operated a successful photographic studio in that city. Eight illustrations in the book have been located in the Notman archives, including one Boorne and May original which is reproduced in the Haddo House collection, and two further Boorne and May photographs which provided the basis for the sketches on pages 219 and 221.[22] Two other photographs have been positively identified from the British Columbia archives, and three more were probably obtained from West Coast photographers.[23]

Overall, *Through Canada with a Kodak* presents a faithful visual diary of the Aberdeens' first journey across the Dominion, incorporating both the formal, posed picture and the casual snapshot permitted by Eastman's new invention. There are, however, three major errors in the annotation of the pictorial record. The photograph on page 25, which is identified as Montreal, is in fact a view of Victoria, British Columbia, looking southwest from Church Hill. The original is located in the British Columbia Photographic Archive, with a copy in the Aberdeens' family album. The Kodak photograph of 'Sir John Abbott, Prime Minister of Canada,' on page 79, is not Abbott, but Sir John Carling, the long-serving minister of agriculture. Perhaps on that occasion Lady Aberdeen did not make a sufficiently careful note of her 'snap' in the memorandum book which was always supplied with Eastman's Kodak cameras! And the sketch on page 136 is based on a professional photograph of Mount Rundle, not Cascade Mountain, Banff.

The Text

Travel writing has been a familiar and popular literary form since time immemorial, ranging from the autobiographical guidebooks of medieval pilgrims to the topographical diaries of explorers, the exhortative accounts of missionaries, and the self-indulgent anecdotes of eighteenth-century 'Grand Tourers.' These and other manifestations of the travelogue all reflect the enduring enthusiasm of writers to record their adventures and of publishers to make them available to a reading public eager for vicarious enjoyment of the travellers' experiences. It was therefore no surprise that the transport revolution of the nineteenth century, with the new opportunities it afforded for emigration and tourism, generated an intensified torrent of travel literature, much of it directed towards the newly accessible continents of America and Australasia.

Discriminating readers and reviewers sometimes regarded the phenomenon as a mixed blessing. As early as 1760, the caustic Samuel Johnson hinted at the mediocrity of many eighteenth-century travelogues when he observed that 'few books disappoint their readers more than the narrations of travellers.'[24] It was a criticism perhaps even more pertinent in the nineteenth century, as output increased steadily in response to public interest in travel and emigration and to growing competition in the promotional travelogue industry. But as time went on, it became increasingly difficult for travel writers to be original; the age of exploration, discovery, and pioneering settlement was largely over, and they often found themselves writing about territories whose history, geography, and scenic attractions had been defined and analysed by their literary predecessors. Indeed, each generation of travellers – and travel writers – was inevitably influenced by the preceding generation's definitions of significant events, places, and concepts, and was therefore predisposed to accept and follow a prescribed itinerary. Travellers who visited and wrote about well-documented locations therefore had to be particularly alert to the pitfalls of plagiarism and hackneyed repetition, and had to make a conscious effort to offer an original interpretation of what they had seen and done.

Many travel writers succeeded admirably in this task, and their idiosyncratic comments on familiar places and events illuminate both their own priorities and the social, economic, political, and cultural background which had shaped those priorities. Such writers, by virtue of what Paul Carter calls 'their active engagement with the road and the horizon,' do not simply describe places or events passively and meaninglessly: their shrewd analysis also makes them active participants in the historical process.[25]

How does *Through Canada with a Kodak* rank in the hierarchy of travelogues? Lady Aberdeen was well aware of the book's limitations. As she readily admitted in her preface, she did 'not aspire to deal with the deeper questions of Canadian life or politics,' and made no claim to present a balanced picture of the Dominion in the 1890s. Many of her observations were, she stressed, little more than superficial impressions, which were no substitute for the considered opinions of long-time residents.[26] Places and topics were highlighted on the basis of her personal interests and experiences rather than in the pursuit of a comprehensive presentation of the condition of Canada. For instance, although the Toronto Fair was described in some detail, the city itself stimulated very little comment, and burgeoning western centres, particularly Calgary, were similarly passed over in favour of graphic accounts of the minutiae of the Aberdeens' daily activities and social intercourse. Contact with ordinary people and everyday events was negligible, for the aristocratic visitors were received at the highest level of Canadian society and their dealings were with the Dominion's political and social élite.

But the book's very selectivity is its greatest strength as well as its main weakness, for in this selectivity lies the all-important quality of originality. Ishbel's written, as well as visual, snapshot of Canadian society in the 1890s reflects her own unique experiences and concerns. In particular it demonstrates the interests of a well-connected visitor who, believing that the attractions of Canada were 'very imperfectly realised' in Britain, sought to remedy that deficiency in a time-honoured and popular way – through the publication of her own edited travel journal. In her very awareness of the manuscript's limitations, she demonstrated a sagacity and perceptiveness which she went on to display throughout the narrative itself. Her unique contribution lay most particularly in her promotion of female immigration and her refreshingly open-minded attitude to travel, while her distinguished background gave her easier access than many other commentators to people and places across the Dominion. Some of her encounters were also of historiographical significance, her optimistic predictions for the infant Killarney colony especially demonstrating her own version of Carter's 'active engagement with the road and the horizon.'[27]

Lady Aberdeen was concerned with conveying her impressions in both words and pictures. *Through Canada with a Kodak* is therefore not only a visual record, but also a perceptive commentary on the contemporary Canadian social and political scene, as well as an edited diary of personal and family experiences. The book opens with a 151-page account of a three-month sojourn in the Dominion in 1890, followed by 47 pages which deal with a shorter visit to British Columbia the following year. It ends with a detailed discussion of the traditions of the Native people and a seven-page appendix commemorating the recently deceased Sir John A. Macdonald. A prolific diarist since the age of thirteen, Ishbel had ample raw material on which to draw in compiling her manuscript, and the availability (in the National Archives of Canada) of her unabridged, unpublished Canadian journal permits detailed comparison of the two texts.[28] Evidence in that source of the author's discreet pruning of her private diary before publication offers a fascinating insight into her priorities, prejudices, and private life, particularly those parts of her private life which she was determined were to remain hidden from the public gaze.

The First Trip

In taking their passage from Liverpool, by far the busiest embarkation port in the British Isles, the Aberdeens followed the same route as the vast majority of transatlantic travellers and emigrants from Britain and Europe throughout the nineteenth century. Under the charge of Captain Ritchie of Ayrshire was a motley shipload of cabin and steerage passengers, the former including a number of Canadian politicians and other public figures, whose acquaintance with the Aberdeens was to be renewed in the Dominion. The much larger steerage contingent included several emigrants who were travelling under the auspices of the Salvation Army, which in this era adopted emigration as an integral part of its welfare program, to the extent that it was recognized as the leading emigration agency in Britain, and perhaps in the world.[29]

The Aberdeens soon discovered that while a cabin passage might afford privacy, it certainly offered no immunity against seasickness, to which most of the 750 passengers aboard the SS *Parisian* succumbed while still in the Irish Sea. Lady Aberdeen was not impressed with the facilities on the much-vaunted *Parisian*, although she chose to confine these views to the pages of her private journal:

I should never advise anyone to come by this boat. In consequence of her reputation everyone makes a rush to come by her, and so every berth is full and the steerage is crammed, the ventilation and sanitary arrangements are defective and the ship is undermanned. Besides this, we have a heavy cargo of iron, and it seems an accepted fact that there are not sufficient boats in case of accident. You should see the cabins where Barron and Turner [two of the servants] were put, although they were paid for as saloon passengers, their berths taken in May and a special request made for their comfort. Barron in a cabin with three others – toilet arrangements for only one – the port never being allowed to be open even when in the river, because so near the water and next the laundry. As one gentleman said, he would not put his dog to sleep in such places.[30]

The miseries of the steerage passengers were even more public, but although they escaped the inquisitive lens of Lady Aberdeen's Kodak, she had plenty of opportunity to observe and comment on their activities. Many, she felt, would never have emigrated if they had been honestly apprised in advance of the discomforts of the voyage: 'I should think the greatest kindness one could do for those poor folk would be to bring a few odd chairs & lots of amusing books & games for them – they are not allowed to use their hammocks by day & so the poor ill ones lie about on the deck anyhow in abject misery & there is nowhere much for anyone to sit on except on the sails.'[31]

Singled out for special comment were the fifty 'Home girls' who were being escorted out 'from misery and destitution' to Maria Rye's Homes at Niagara-on-the-Lake, and then on to adoption or employment in Canadian homes.[32] Lady Aberdeen was an enthusiastic advocate of the controversial Home Children movement, which between 1869 and 1930 brought to Canada around one hundred thousand unaccompanied, often destitute, British children from the age of three upwards. Part of the late Victorian web of evangelical philanthropy herself, she was well acquainted with the leading pioneers of assisted juvenile migration. Maria Rye had been taking girls to Niagara-on-the-Lake since 1869, despite an unfavourable official report on her activities in 1874.[33] Annie Macpherson, who operated three receiving homes in Quebec and Ontario (and whom the Aberdeens were later to meet on the train to Winnipeg), sent her first contingent in 1870; and Dr Thomas Barnardo, who ultimately became the biggest and most controversial child emigrationist, made use of Annie Macpherson's reception facilities for ten years until he developed his own system in 1882. But probably most familiar to Lady Aberdeen were the activities of William Quarrier, whose Orphan Homes of Scotland despatched almost seven thousand children to Canada between 1872 and 1930. Indeed, young women sent to Canada under the auspices of her Aberdeen Ladies' Union – whose commitment to emigration was itself an adaptation of the 'Home Children' concept – were transported initially under the auspices of Quarrier's Homes.[34]

Having given the obligatory account of the sighting of their first iceberg, Lady Aberdeen described briefly the ship's progress up the St Lawrence, past 'dear wee tin-roofed cottages & red-roofed churches.'[35] The *Parisian* docked at Quebec City after a nine-day voyage, though not before Lord Aberdeen had incurred Captain Ritchie's wrath by presenting to him a round robin from the passengers voicing their complaints about facilities on the ship. Most of the passengers disembarked at Quebec City, and Miss Rye's charges, Lady Aberdeen noted optimistically, boarded their Niagara-bound train 'very happily.'[36] Both at Quebec City and at Montreal Lady Aberdeen was at pains to investigate and report on the reception facilities for that category of assisted settlers in which she had a more personal and professional interest, facilities provided by the Women's Protective Immigration Society and the Home for Female Emigrants respectively. Indeed, her advice to female emigrants regarding travel, reception, and well-remunerated employment opportunities took precedence over her general impressions of Quebec City, and set the tone for much of the book. After all, the investigation of opportunities for emigrants was a prime reason for her visit to Canada, and it was a theme to which she returned regularly throughout the trip.

But Ishbel was also a tourist and did not neglect to sample – and appraise – all the main tourist attractions of the Dominion, from Quebec City to Vancouver Island. Ever since Wolfe's victory over Montcalm in 1759, Quebec City had been a source of fascination to British travellers in Canada, and the Plains of Abraham a required place of pilgrimage. As a result, by 1893 French Canada was frequently a victim of romantic stereotyping in British literature. Histories and travelogues painted it as a quaint but backward enclave of Roman Catholicism, and restructured its traditions and heritage to fit an image of superior and magnanimous British imperialism. Lady Aberdeen's comments on both Quebec City and Montreal clearly reflect this erroneous and rather patronizing interpretation of French Canada's history and culture. Looking down from her vantage point in the Citadel on a Quebec City skyline, whose Gothic spires and French chateaux buildings were largely the creation of nineteenth-century advocates of medieval architecture, she reflected on the exploits of chivalric heroes of old – Cartier, Champlain, and subsequently the 'daring' Wolfe and his 'noble-hearted' enemy.[37] Contemporary French Canadians were depicted as bucolic, respectful, but backward peasants, whose steadfast loyalty to the British Crown had been secured by British toleration of their religion and customs after the conquest of Quebec. But although such stereotypes were a common feature of late

Victorian writing, images of French Canada as a conservative rural backwater untouched by modern civilization did not accord with the realities of urbanization, industrialization, and nascent Quebec nationalism. These realities Lady Aberdeen either did not perceive or chose to ignore.[38]

This fascination with ancient French-Canadian society was also evident during a three-day stopover at Montreal, where Lady Aberdeen reflected nostalgically on the 'nestling Indian village' founded by Jacques Cartier and on the adventures of Sieur de Maisonneuve, who was the first governor of Montreal, from 1642 to 1665. She was less impressed with contemporary French-Canadian politicians, namely the Quebec premier, Honoré Mercier, who had accompanied them on part of the train journey from Quebec City to Montreal, and whom she described – privately – as 'v. French in all ways, & does not inspire one with confidence.'[39] At Montreal, where they stayed at the 900-bed Windsor Hotel, the Aberdeens' schedule included an ascent of the mountain, a tour of the Female Emigrants' Home, and a visit to a family friend before they continued westwards to meet their children and household servants at Hamilton.

Lord and Lady Aberdeens' experiences, of course, were not representative, for, unlike the ordinary traveller or emigrant, they stayed in the most prestigious residences and constantly rubbed shoulders with the political and social élite of the Dominion. Perhaps Lady Aberdeen's most enduring memory of her visit to Montreal was the evening spent at the home of Sir Donald Smith, the venerable Scot who, after emigrating from Forres in Morayshire in 1838, had spent twenty years in the service of the Hudson's Bay Company in the frozen wastes of Labrador. By 1890 he was Governor of the Company and actively involved in both Dominion politics and railway investment, having largely masterminded the financing of the Canadian Pacific Railway's construction in the previous decade.[40] Other luminaries entertained by Smith that evening included Thomas Shaughnessy, Vice-President (subsequently President) of the CPR, Edinburgh-born James Barclay, minister of St Paul's Presbyterian Church, Montreal, from 1883 until his retirement in 1910, and Albert Lacombe, pioneer Roman Catholic missionary to the Indians and Métis of the Northwest Territories. In an evening of storytelling, Lady Aberdeen was particularly enthralled by Lacombe's and Barclay's tales of evangelistic work among the Native people, and she subsequently devoted the final section of the guidebook to discussing her impressions of the Indians of Canada.[41]

From Montreal the Aberdeens continued by train to Côteau, where they boarded the *Corsican*, under its English-born captain, for the river and lake trip westwards to Toronto. They made full use of a two-hour stopover at Kingston, where their first priority was to visit Annie Smith, the daughter of one of Lord Aberdeen's tenants, whom they had sent out two years earlier and who had not been keeping in touch with her family in Scotland. Despite the birth of an illegitimate child, she was found to be still in domestic service with her original employer, 'who continues to give her a v. good character indeed.'[42] Annie's satisfaction with her situation reinforced Lady Aberdeen's faith in Canada as a haven for 'the right sort of hard-working girls,' and she secured a promise from Kingston's chief Presbyterian minister, Dr Mackie, that he would take a pastoral interest in this rather wayward recruit.

Having done their duty, the Aberdeens then indulged in a tour of the sights of Kingston under the guidance of an Irish cab-driver, and had afternoon tea at the hotel before re-embarking on the *Corsican* for the journey along Lake Ontario. But they were soon to regret the decision not to take the train, for the weather, which had already prevented a trip to Lachine Rapids and had marred their cruise through the Thousand Islands the previous day, worsened again that evening, until at 3 a.m., the captain agreed to let his distinguished passengers abandon ship at Cobourg. From there, with the help of the aptly named steamboat agent, Mr Cruso, they managed to intercept the night train to Toronto two hours later.

At this juncture Lord and Lady Aberdeen did not linger in Toronto but continued straight through to Hamilton, where, through the good offices of the governor general, Lord Stanley, and his son, along with Senator W.E. Sanford of Hamilton, they had secured accommodation for the duration of their visit to Ontario. Their request had posed 'rather a problem,' according to Eddie Stanley, for:

hotels are so bad on this continent that I should advise taking a house, but furnished houses are a rarity. For Canada unlike Australia has no rich people, and hence few large houses. Ottawa would be far too hot in August, and Quebec too cold for children in October, but at Hamilton ... the temperature is nice all the year round. And I think I have found a house there to suit you, Highfield, with 15 acres, good rides and under a mile from the Lake; they would take 1,000 dollars – £200 – for the three months, which is decidedly cheap.[43]

The Aberdeens were well pleased with Highfield, where they were reunited with their four children and their full entourage of staff, eight of whom were to remain in Canada as permanent settlers. Hamilton's United Empire Loyalist past, and its burgeoning industrial, commercial, and cultural present impressed Lady Aberdeen, although she admitted privately that 'our public appearances ... such as going to church are rather painful, and decidedly comical. We are so evidently

Introduction to the 1994 Edition xlv

regarded as belonging to a Museum of Curiosities.'[44] Family recreation took the form of nocturnal moth-hunting expeditions in the grounds of Highfield, during which illuminated trees and telegraph poles were smeared with a mixture of molasses and honey in order to entrap as many unwary victims as possible.

The visit to Hamilton was not allowed to pass without a trip to Niagara Falls, which for over a century had been the mecca of the nascent Canadian tourist industry. While a small élite of aristocratic eighteenth-century travellers had publicized the romantic attractions of the Falls in word and sketch, it was not until the opening of the Erie Canal in 1825 that substantial numbers of middle-class visitors were able to experience Niagara's wonders for themselves. By that time the romantic rapture engendered by the natural grandeur of the cataract could be reinforced by the 'pleasant sensation of sadness' inspired by the battle-sites of the 1812 War and veneration of the gallant achievements of General Brock.[45] Visitors flocked to experience the various aesthetic pleasures of the Niagara frontier, their expectations of an intense emotional experience heightened by the romantic rhetoric of a bewildering array of guidebooks, travel journals, and poetry. The subsequent disappointment of many that the reality did not correspond to the preconceived image may have been largely the fault of the increasingly commercialized amenities which had developed to cater to their needs. It is indeed ironic that the tourist industry which had been created out of the romantic appeal of Niagara ultimately – but perhaps inevitably – destroyed that appeal, domesticating the wilderness with intrusive marketing, and forcing the true romantic traveller to seek his sublime aesthetic experience elsewhere.

By the time the Aberdeens visited Canada in 1890, blatant, competitive commercialism had almost entirely supplanted the primitive romanticism of the Niagara frontier. Perhaps for this reason, the obligatory visit to the Falls did not inspire Lady Aberdeen to the lengthy description and adulation favoured by so many diarists, who, in her view, had exhausted the dictionary in eulogizing the cataract. She confined herself to the observation – made by many travel writers – that the natural splendour of Niagara could only be experienced personally, never conveyed by written description, and her diary records no other impressions of the Niagara frontier.

Instead she passed over this part of the visit in order to highlight the various public duties undertaken by her husband during their time in Ontario, including opening the Hamilton Library and the autumn fairs at London and (particularly) Toronto. Hospitality in the latter city was provided by Sir Alexander Campbell, 'a dear old gentleman,' lieutenant-governor of Ontario, and one of several dignitaries from that province who had been among the Aberdeens' fellow-passengers on the transatlantic crossing.[46] The political atmosphere of Government House was meat and drink to Lady Aberdeen, who relished debating Canadian politics with Oliver Mowat, the Liberal prime minister of Ontario, George W. Allan, Speaker of the Dominion Senate, and Edward Blake, former Liberal prime minister of Ontario, who in 1890 had just withdrawn from active politics.[47]

The opportunity for political debate was continued at a higher level when the Aberdeens visited Ottawa and made the acquaintance of several Dominion politicians, including Sir John A. Macdonald, the Scots-born architect of Confederation and first prime minister of the Dominion of Canada. Indeed, wherever they went the Aberdeens were struck by the large number of successful Scottish settlers at all levels of society, from the prime minister and the president of the CPR to the Hebridean homesteaders on the Manitoba prairies, and the various emigrants from Aberdeenshire who were forging new careers across Western Canada. While in the capital they also visited a sawmill, purchased a pair of carriage horses at the Ottawa Fair, and were subsequently taken by Sir John Carling, the minister of agriculture – whom they had met at the fair – to visit the government experimental farm just outside the city. Little did they realize, as they paid their respects at Rideau Hall, that within three years they themselves would be taking up its tenancy, and entering upon the centre-stage of Ottawa's political and social life, when Lord Aberdeen took up the office of governor general.

During their parents' excursions to Toronto and Ottawa, the children had been left at Highfield in the charge of a governess. With the exception of Lord Haddo, who returned to school in England, they remained in Hamilton while Lord and Lady Aberdeen set out from Ottawa on the next stage of their tour – a railway trip to Vancouver in a luxurious private car provided by Sir Donald Smith and the CPR, complete with white mahogany fittings, a separate dining car, and a black porter. The Canadian Pacific Company, Lady Aberdeen assured her readers, did everything well, 'whether it concerns the piercing of the Rocky Mountains or the making of good soup.'[48] She did not reflect on whether the immigrant occupants of the train's two 'colonist cars,' who had to provide their own food and mattresses, would have endorsed that commendation.

The Aberdeens were now leaving behind the relatively mature, settled society of eastern Canada, and heading west to the region which since the 1870s had been capturing the attention of so many immigrants, travellers, and propagandists as the focus of future Canadian settlement and prosperity. Among their fellow-passengers was Annie Macpherson, the Scottish child

Introduction to the 1994 Edition xlix

emigrationist, with whom Lady Aberdeen had a 'long talk' about the advantages of bringing destitute children – and destitute Scottish crofters – to Canada.[49] Their first stop, five hours behind schedule, was Winnipeg, where Sir Donald Smith had put his 'dear little snug house,' the inaptly-named 'Silver Heights,' at their disposal for the duration of their visit.[50] Here they were visited not only by the leading citizens of Winnipeg, but also by Lady Aberdeen's wayward remittance-man brother, Coutts Marjoribanks, who 'rejoiced our hearts by turning up from Dakota.'[51] Coutts was not making a financial success of managing his father's 1,260-acre Horseshoe Ranch at Towner, North Dakota, and it was Ishbel's wish that he should cut his losses and move to Canada that partly underlay Lord Aberdeen's subsequent surprise decision to purchase ranchland in British Columbia.[52]

Lady Aberdeen was favourably impressed with the citizens of Winnipeg, but not with the city itself or its environs. Winnipeg bore all the hallmarks of recent, haphazard growth:

The houses are sort of scattered as yet pell mell as if you had thrown them down in a handful, a big one and then a little old log hut by the side of it and then a store and so on and of course weeds everywhere. There is a good City Hall – the Parliament Buildings lately put up look substantial and unpretentious but when you look down on the city from the Tower of Government House there seems but one building in Winnipeg, and that is an enormous red hotel which is being put up by the Northern Pacific Co.[53]

For many immigrants, Winnipeg was simply the place where they broke their journey and registered a claim to a prairie homestead which they then sought to locate. Lured out to Manitoba by agents' promises of boundless opportunities in the 'Golden West,' they were often ill-prepared for the bleakness and remoteness of their new settlements, and Lady Aberdeen could well appreciate the disillusionment of settlers whose experiences bore no relationship to their expectations. She too found the prairies repellent:

May Heaven preserve us from ever being fated to banishment to the far-famed wheatlands of Manitoba. Oh the inexpressible dreariness of these everlasting prairies, with their serpentine black trails winding through them – the only objects standing out being little untidy-looking corn-ricks and wooden shanties, most of the size which would be put up as a keeper's shelter at home but here inhabited often by farmers owning some hundreds of acres and some half-dozen or dozen children ... the struggle to live has swallowed up all the energy, and it has been quite the exception to see even any attempt after the commonest form of tidiness, much less any attempt to nurture a few flowers or plant a tree. One would not think that such a life could be helpful in fostering any higher tendencies.[54]

Introduction to the 1994 Edition

It was in an attempt to brighten the drab lives of these homesteaders – particularly the women – that Lady Aberdeen spearheaded the formation of the Winnipeg-based 'Aberdeen Association for the Distribution of Literature to Settlers in the West.' On her way back from British Columbia a month later, she again stopped in Winnipeg, where she addressed a 1,400-strong women's meeting at Knox Church. Having recalled her distress at the homesteaders' plight, she urged her audience to organize local collections of suitable magazines, books, and newspapers and at regular intervals to despatch parcels of this reading material, along with flower seeds and small ornaments, to isolated prairie homesteads. So was born the Aberdeen Association, whose members – initially only in Winnipeg but before long in other cities across both Canada and Britain – corresponded regularly with hundreds of prairie settlers right up until the First World War. The British public was apprised of the scheme by the newspaper and periodical press, as well as through the pages of *Onward and Upward* and *Through Canada with a Kodak*, while Lady Aberdeen persuaded a number of transatlantic shipping companies, and the CPR, to transport the literature parcels free of charge.[55]

Lady Aberdeen's concern for the welfare of prairie settlers was precipitated partly by her spontaneous visits to former 'Onward and Upward' girls who were working on homesteads and ranches across Manitoba, the North-west Territories and British Columbia, sometimes in locations up to fifty miles distant from the railway. But she was also profoundly influenced by an official trip organized, during her first Winnipeg stopover, to the infant Scottish settlement at Killarney.

The Killarney colony, and a similar settlement at Saltcoats, in the Northwest Territories, was part of an attempt to solve long-standing problems of overpopulation and land hunger in the Scottish Highlands. At the beginning of the nineteenth century landlords had considered a large labour force essential to the modernization of their estates. But they soon found these tenants an expensive liability as the Highland economy nosedived after the Napoleonic Wars and as the region began to lurch through repeated subsistence crises. In their efforts to avoid bankruptcy, landlords pursued a policy of clearance, turning more and more land over to incoming sheep farmers and evicting the displaced tenants either to peripheral crofts or off the estates entirely. Some landlords helped their tenants to emigrate to Canada, while charitable relief agencies organized subsidized passages to Australia in the 1840s and 1850s. Pleas for state-aided emigration – or, indeed, for any government intervention in the Highlands – generally fell on deaf ears, despite continuing problems of congestion and pauperism, particularly on the western seaboard and in the Hebridean islands. Only in the 1880s, after the crofters' frustration at arbitrary eviction and inequitable land distribution had erupted in prolonged and widespread violence (the so-called Crofters' War) did the government take decisive action. In 1886, acting on the recommendations of a Royal Commission appointed to examine the crofters' grievances, legislation was passed which gave crofters, for the first time, a measure of security of tenure, and set a precedent for much greater government intervention in the Highlands thereafter.[56]

Yet problems of congestion remained, particularly in the Outer Hebrides. Instead of redistributing the land, as the crofters and landless cottars wished, the government listened to the proprietors, and, in 1888, agreed to finance a small-scale emigration scheme in the hope of defusing continuing economic and social tension. A government grant of £10,000 was to be supplemented by £2,000 raised by private subscription, in order to settle one hundred crofting families from Lewis, Harris, and North Uist on prairie homesteads at Killarney and Saltcoats. Loans of £120 were to be made to each family, to be repaid in instalments out of profits made from working the homestead, which itself provided security for the loan. Contrary to Marjorie Pentland's subsequent claim that her father had donated £2,000 to this colonization fund, the money was in fact raised partly by Highland landlords, who raised £700 in response to a personal appeal from Lord Lothian, the Scottish Secretary, and partly by donations from public meetings, primarily in Glasgow, which raised £1,300.[57] Lord and Lady Aberdeen had no financial interest in the project, and neither in her published nor private writings did Ishbel mention any such donation made by her husband. Their visit to Killarney, described in detail in *Through Canada with a Kodak*, was probably arranged simply in order to satisfy their curiosity about the progress of this much-publicized settlement, which only two weeks earlier had been visited by a delegation of British tenant farmers sponsored by the Dominion government. The photographic record supports this suggestion, for the colony appears to have attracted the attention of professional photographers as well as Lady Aberdeen with her Kodak. Indeed, Lady Aberdeen may well have obtained some of her photographs of Killarney from Thomas Mills of Bangor, North Wales, a professional photographer who was hired by the Canadian High Commission to accompany the farmer delegates and publicize their tour.[58]

When the Aberdeens visited the two-year-old Killarney settlement in 1890, they were confident that its teething troubles had been overcome, and that the colonists were well on their way to prosperity. In fact, such predictions were premature. Many of the Hebridean crofter-fishermen were unwilling or unable to adapt to life on a prairie homestead, and often preferred to work as seasonal harvest labourers or railway navvies, rather

Introduction to the 1994 Edition   lv

than settle down to cultivate their quarter-sections. At both Killarney and Saltcoats their tardiness in paying Canadian taxes and repaying their £120 loans to the British government discouraged any extension of the scheme, and from the official perspective, both settlements rapidly became expensive embarrassments. At the same time, unfavourable publicity from the colonists about ill-prepared locations and inadequate loans turned their compatriots still in the Highlands even more firmly against emigration, and intensified their demands that government grants should be channelled into economic development at home, rather than into futile and unpopular colonization projects.[59]

Despite her confident predictions of success, and her enthusiastic 'kodaking' of the sometimes camera-shy Hebridean settlers, Lady Aberdeen was eager to get away from Killarney and the 'everlasting prairies.' But shortly after resuming their train journey, the engine collided with a herd of cattle thirty-five miles west of Winnipeg, derailing several carriages and destroying a section of track. Injuries were few, however, and the passengers resumed their journey the following day – though not before Lady Aberdeen had made full use of her opportunity to sketch and photograph the wreck. As they travelled west through yet more featureless, deserted terrain, her aversion to the prairies was confirmed, yet at the same time, she was convinced by the assurances of several fellow-passengers that in the 'black mud' of Manitoba and the Northwest Territories lay the future prosperity of Canada and its new immigrants. Among these immigrants she was particularly interested in a number from Aberdeenshire, including one John Will from the village of Methlick, just north of Haddo House. Will, who until then had been labouring for thirty dollars a month on one of the large southern Alberta ranches of the British investor, Sir John Lister-Kaye, was about to buy his own farm near Edmonton. There he was to be joined by his Aberdeenshire bride, a Haddo House Associate, although when she subsequently died only a few months after their marriage, Will moved to British Columbia to work on Lord Aberdeen's newly acquired ranches.[60]

Having lost almost twenty-four hours because of the derailment, Lady Aberdeen was by now impatient to reach the West Coast. A proposed stop at Calgary was cancelled, and the new towns and untapped resources of Alberta were dismissed in a few sentences, alongside a brief review of the exploits of the Hudson's Bay Company in the region. Only when the train reached the foothills of the Rockies did her spirits really rise, and she confessed in her journal that she would have wished to linger in the mountains:

Do you know what it is to be surfeited with beautiful scenery? We have been in that case to-day. All day long from Canmore to Banff, up the Rockies, through the Selkirks, along the Columbia, through the Kicking Horse Pass, Roger's Pass under the shade of Sir Donald till the departing light found us at Glacier House & left us there at dinner, how we rushed about from side to side, & from end to end of the carriage, vainly attempting, if not to photograph or sketch, at least to imprint some memory of what we saw. Well it is all a jumble now, & we can but uselessly regret not having days to give to each place. I vote for this region for the shanty wh. A. is so anxious to erect on Canadian soil.[61]

Only one halt was made, at the Banff Springs Hotel, opened by the CPR two years earlier and modelled on a Scottish castle.[62] A chance meeting at Banff with the daughter of yet another of Lord Aberdeen's tenants gave Ishbel a further opportunity to indulge in imperialist rhetoric about the large numbers of successful Scots in Canada, not least those who had masterminded the construction of the 'wonderful railway' on which she was travelling.

Lady Aberdeen's impatience to reach the West Coast was due to her long-anticipated rendezvous with the Scottish theologian Henry Drummond, a family friend and probably her lover from at least 1884 until his death in 1897.[63] Her private journal both on this trip and on her following visit to North America in 1891 was addressed jointly to Drummond and his close friend John Sinclair, Lord Aberdeen's aide-de-camp and subsequently Lady Marjorie Gordon's husband, although on both occasions Drummond's name appeared first in the dedication.[64] While the Aberdeens travelled west by the CPR, Drummond had been making his way to Canada via Australia, Japan, and San Francisco, keeping Ishbel informed of his progress by regular letters and telegrams. Outwardly circumspect, Ishbel omitted any ambiguous reference to Drummond from her published writings, but was less inhibited when making entries in her private journal. On 20 September, while still in Hamilton, she had written that her 'spirits [were] greatly revived by a telegram from Yokohama saying that H.D. starts next Thursday for Frisco ... it will be real good to see him – we were beginning to chafe at not hearing from him & to long greatly for a sign of life.' And on hearing subsequently of Henry's arrival at San Francisco, en route for Vancouver, she wrote with eager anticipation: 'So at last we are on the same continent and shall get nearer one another hour by hour.'[65]

In order to expedite the reunion with Drummond, the Aberdeens went straight from the railway terminus at Vancouver to the ferry, even though it was Sunday and by the time they reached Victoria everything was shut up and most of the citizens were abed. The following day – designated a 'Red Letter Day' in Ishbel's private journal – was taken up with a round of public engagements in the company of the Irish-born governor, Hugh

Nelson, and the English-born former governor, Sir Joseph Trutch. Like so many visitors to Victoria, Ishbel was struck by the distinct English flavour of the society, and was further convinced that hard-working domestic servants from the 'Old Country' could not fail to succeed in the West, as well as in eastern Canada. Drummond arrived from Tacoma in time for an evening reception at Government House, during which Mrs Nelson – prophetically – told Lady Aberdeen 'much about the ways of Governors General and their wives.'[66] To the chagrin of their hosts, the party then boarded the night ferry for Vancouver, in order to accommodate Drummond's requirement to take a transatlantic passage from New York on 26 October.

Vancouver, like Victoria, was allocated only one day in the itinerary. After a drive around the city sights and a 'rather prolonged luncheon' in the company of the mayor and his wife, the Aberdeens turned their minds to business – in particular, the purchase of a property on which to settle Lady Aberdeen's brother Coutts. They had arranged a meeting with a Scottish acquaintance, George Grant MacKay, an engineer who had once constructed roads at Guisachan, the Inverness-shire estate of Lady Aberdeen's father. A former real-estate dealer in the Scottish Highlands, MacKay had come to Canada in 1887, having found 'that land at home was getting to be a rather bad business.'[67] By 1890 he had established real-estate companies both in Vancouver and in the Okanagan Valley, so when the Aberdeens demurred at the price of improved farms in the Fraser Valley, he was not slow to tell them about the excellent prospects for commercial fruit-farming in the Okanagan. The consequence was that before they left Vancouver the Aberdeens commissioned MacKay to purchase a 480-acre property in the Okanagan Valley, which they named Guisachan Ranch, about which Lady Aberdeen was to write at length in subsequent chapters of *Through Canada with a Kodak*.

The following day the Aberdeens, along with Drummond, boarded the train for the return journey to the East. With her departure from the West Coast Lady Aberdeen closed the public record of her first trip to Canada, although in editing her journal for publication as *Through Canada with a Kodak*, she in fact conflated several incidents which had occurred on the outward and return journeys.[68] After making short halts at Banff and Medicine Hat, the party proceeded to Winnipeg, where all three had public engagements, and where Ishbel inaugurated the Aberdeen Association. Then, with Coutts in tow, they continued eastwards, Lord Aberdeen to Ottawa, and the others to rejoin the children in Hamilton, before they all met up at Highfield and travelled to New York to take their passage for Liverpool on the SS *Umbria*. Throughout this final leg of the tour, all

Introduction to the 1994 Edition   lxi

the party's activities seem to have been tailored to fit Drummond's interests, and it is perhaps appropriate that the published record of the 1890 trip should conclude with a 'kodak' of Drummond and the long-suffering Lord Aberdeen, eastward-bound on the CPR.

The Second Trip

In September 1891 Lord and Lady Aberdeen, accompanied by their ten-year-old daughter, Marjorie, returned to North America. Their three-month visit began and ended in the United States. From New York, where they disembarked, they travelled north to Canada, taking in a visit to Drummond's evangelist friend Dwight Moody en route. In both Montreal and Ottawa they stayed in the same hotels as on their previous trip, revisited old haunts, and renewed old friendships. In Ottawa they moved mainly in political circles, making the acquaintance of Sir John Abbott, who had replaced Macdonald as prime minister following the latter's death in June 1891. But although her thoughts on the Canadian political and social scene were recorded in detail in her journal, on this occasion Ishbel was not concerned with giving her *Onward and Upward* readers a blow-by-blow account of the entire trip. Glossing over both her activities in eastern Canada, and her train trip through the 'dreary alkaline prairie lands,'[69] she opened her published reminiscences with a brief reference to the family's ten-day halt at Banff, where they spent their time sketching, riding, and swimming, and trying to avoid public engagements. After persistent efforts, they also met Sir John A. Macdonald's widow, Lady Agnes, who had been reluctant at first to acknowledge their presence on the grounds of their fervent Liberalism and support for Gladstone.

The real focus of the family's attention, however, was a nine-day visit to their new British Columbia home. At Sicamous Junction they left the main CPR route to travel forty-six miles south to Vernon on the first passenger train to run on the still unopened Shuswap and Okanagan branch line. Having chartered a special train, and having encountered yet another emigrant from the Haddo estate at a farm en route, they arrived in Vernon in time to see Guisachan Ranch take twelve prizes in the district's first agricultural show. Accompanied by Coutts, who met them in Vernon, they then boarded the lake steamer to travel a further thirty-five miles south to their property at Kelowna. To Lady Aberdeen's delight, the topography, which she had expected to be flat and scrubby, reminded her very much of her family's holiday home in the Scottish Highlands, and she immediately fell in love with Guisachan.

British Columbia's growing popularity with wealthy 'gentlemen emigrants' in the late nineteenth century was due largely to its reputation as a sportsman's paradise. When the Aberdeens had purchased Guisachan a year earlier, Ishbel had noted in her journal George MacKay's assurance that it was 'on a plateau surrounded by hills where the most splendid sport can be had,'[70] and the family now had the opportunity to put that assurance to the test. On the day after their arrival they participated in an unsuccessful bear hunt, and seemed to spend much of the following week shooting anything that moved. Some of their hunting expeditions were undertaken in the company of the ranch's international workforce, which included English, Scots, Canadians, Americans, and Chinese. The visitors were also warmly welcomed by their neighbours, and Lady Aberdeen was at particular pains to stress the careful provision that had been made for religious services, both Protestant and Roman Catholic. Indeed, so impressed were the Aberdeens with the Okanagan that, at the end of their brief visit, they made another, more extensive purchase, the 13,261-acre Coldstream Ranch at the northern end of the valley. This property was bought, along with two thousand cattle, seventy horses, pigs, implements, crops, hay, and furniture, at a cost of £49,000 from the Irish pioneer Forbes Vernon, and after the Aberdeens had left Guisachan, Coutts Marjoribanks moved north to manage his brother-in-law's newly acquired ranch.

But, as Ishbel made clear in her writings, the Okanagan properties were not regarded simply as holiday residences. Lord Aberdeen also had major ambitions for his ranches, proposals which he believed would benefit the local community as well as bring profit to himself. Many people in the Okanagan Valley felt their future prosperity depended on the large ranchers' willingness to subdivide their properties in order to create for sale compact fruit farms of twenty to a hundred acres. This trend was actively encouraged by land companies such as MacKay's, and the Scottish land agent had little difficulty in persuading Lord Aberdeen of the benefit he would confer on the district if he would buy Coldstream and subdivide its large acreage into compact fruit lots.

Part of the new property was in fact entrusted to MacKay, who was to plant orchards and hop yards on a large scale, and sell off the best land in small plots to buyers who wanted to go in for intensive farming and/or fruit growing. By the time of MacKay's death in January 1893, two hundred acres at Coldstream, and a similar area at Guisachan, had been planted with fruit trees, and Lord Aberdeen had also arranged for the construction of a fruit-processing factory in Vernon. Ishbel, ever anxious to promote immigration to Canada, recommended fruit growing to small capitalists and ambitious labourers, whose settlement would benefit the Valley both commercially and socially. Confident that huge profits were just around the corner, the Aberdeens continued to pour money into tree planting, irrigation, and ancillary activities throughout the 1890s, despite repeated warnings from accountants and agricultural experts that mismanagement and excessive expenditure were bringing the ranches to the verge of financial ruin. Only in 1903, after more than a decade of deficits, did Lord Aberdeen sell Guisachan and incorporate his Coldstream property, in which he remained a shareholder until 1921.

Although the optimism reflected in *Through Canada with a Kodak* was to evaporate in the face of repeated failures of crops, markets, and personnel, the Aberdeens' Okanagan Valley investment was not a total disaster. Despite his lack of personal success Lord Aberdeen still made a positive contribution to the Valley's development. He was long remembered in the area as the most committed of the pioneer investors who changed the direction of the region's economy from extensive cattle ranching to intensive fruit farming, in the process promoting employment and a steady influx of British settlers. It is ironic that the establishment of the Okanagan as one of Canada's major fruit-growing regions was due largely to his pioneering initiative, yet was accomplished at the expense of his own investments in the area and to the severe financial embarrassment of his Scottish estates, which supplied much of the capital for the British Columbia experiment.[71]

With the family's departure from British Columbia,

Lady Aberdeen closed her public account of their North American trip. From Vancouver they returned to the United States, where they spent some time in Chicago making arrangements for an elaborate Irish exhibit at the forthcoming World Fair in 1893, and also visited Boston and Washington before embarking at New York on the *City of Paris* for the voyage back to Liverpool. None of these activities was recorded in *Through Canada with a Kodak*, the final section of which was devoted to a lengthy discussion of the manners and customs of the Indians of Canada and a short tribute to the late Sir John A. Macdonald.

Impressions of the Native People

By making observations on the Native people of Canada, Lady Aberdeen was adhering to the pattern of many late Victorian guidebooks, in which this kind of discussion was generally a standard feature of the narrative. Ever since the time of Columbus, European colonists and traders had been fascinated by the mysterious figure of the 'red man,' who by the 1890s starred as hero, villain, or anthropological curiosity in numerous travel accounts, newspaper and magazine articles, school texts, novels, poems, and tracts. Interpreting this voluminous literature was far from straightforward, for the Indian perplexed, as well as fascinated, travellers and writers, who wrestled with a complex kaleidoscope of conflicting images and stereotypes. Readers exposed to these paradoxical images were more likely to be confused than enlightened in their understanding of North American Indians, and Lady Aberdeen's analysis reflects the ambivalent attitudes of her age as well as the more general contemporary interest in the red man on both sides of the border.

The basic issue was whether the Indian should be admired as hero or despised and feared as villain. Should settlers and travellers be attracted or repelled by his presence? Should Indian culture be preserved or eradicated? These issues had, in different guises, provoked debate since the earliest days of European colonization, and no consensus was ever reached. It was a debate complicated by the constantly changing political and cultural backgrounds and motives of the commentators, and by the frequent contradictions within their own arguments, which compounded the more straightforward disparities between image and experience.

The sixteenth-century vision of America as a Garden of Eden inhabited by superior beings whose example could redeem a decadent Europe soon gave way to colonists' accounts of Native savagery and heathenism, and to a seventeenth-century rationalism which relegated the Indian to an almost subhuman position. Their subsequent rehabilitation as 'noble savages' under the influence of eighteenth-century romanticism was in turn challenged on two very different fronts. On the one hand, the rising tide of evangelicalism, with its emphasis on the total depravity of man, and the impossibility of his redemption by any other means than through acceptance of the Christian gospel, discredited the optimistic pantheism of romanticists who portrayed the Indians as the godlike inhabitants of an unsullied Eden. On the other hand, a new cult of realism and materialism repudiated the fantastic images of Rousseau and Chateaubriand because they were so much at variance with both the reports of travellers and settlers and the sentiments of a new utilitarian age. But as the nineteenth century progressed, the zeal of missionaries and utilitarians alike was tempered by a growing anthropological interest in Indians and unease about the anticipated extinction of a whole race of people at the hands of unthinking, land-hungry Europeans.

Positive and negative views of Indians jostled for position in an incessant flow of literature. Glorification of the red man and his land in the romantic novel was displaced by the gruesome but vastly popular 'captivity narratives' of the late eighteenth century and the subsequent novels of Robert Montgomery Bird. James Fenimore Cooper's more charitable representations of Indians were challenged by the writings of disillusioned travellers who had anticipated demi-paradise but found squalor and degradation. Christian commentators agonized over the seemingly impossible task of converting the red man without destroying his civilization, and Utilitarians tried to reconcile their prejudice against Indians as a hindrance to civilized settlement with the need to harness the red man's skills in the practical achievement of that settlement.[72]

A glance through a popular periodical like *Chambers' Journal* reveals both that North American Indians – real and fictional – still made good copy in the late nineteenth century, and that the conflicting stereotypes and moral dilemmas of an earlier age remained largely unresolved.[73] It was therefore no surprise not only that Lady Aberdeen should tackle the subject, but also that she should display in her narrative some of the conflicting stereotypes in which the nineteenth-century reading public had been so thoroughly steeped. Like many of her contemporaries, she was concerned at the visible plight of the Native people, increasing numbers of whom were being condemned to an impoverished, demoralized existence on government reserves, dependent on charity and susceptible to the white man's diseases and the white man's vices. Reflecting on the extent to which this situation had been brought about by the relentless westward march of white settlement, she deplored the thoughtless destruction of the Indians' land, food supply, and dignity, the blame for which she laid largely at the feet of avaricious European colonists. Faced with such economic acquisitiveness and cultural arrogance, it was, she mused, 'small wonder that the red man looks sad, and listless, and hopeless, as he looks out on the altered conditions of life for his race, and as he meditates on the future of his country, which seems to have so little place for him unless he alters all his habits and tastes!'[74]

Ishbel's comments were based on her passing observations of Indians in several parts of Canada, but perhaps her sympathy was stimulated particularly by a conversation she had at Banff in 1891 with the Calgary photographers Boorne and May, who had made a particular study of the Native people of that region. Several of their exquisite photographs, only a few of which appear in *Through Canada with a Kodak*, are preserved in Ishbel's personal album of Canadian illustrations at Haddo House, along with many of the Indian curios acquired in Victoria in 1890 and represented in the sketches by J. Grant.[75] Recognizing that the popular perception of Indians in Britain was often based on nothing more than juvenile adventure stories about ferocious savages, or the fleeting impressions of travellers like herself, Ishbel welcomed the undertaking of serious anthropological studies into the fast-disappearing lifestyle and traditions of the different tribes. She devoted some considerable space to third-party descriptions of the Indians' religious

Introduction to the 1994 Edition lxxi

traditions and ceremonies, oratorical skills, and complex social organization, all presented in a largely straightforward, non-judgmental style. The Aberdeens had themselves witnessed an Indian 'pot-latch' – or ceremonial presentation of gifts – in British Columbia, and although Lord Aberdeen had been rebuffed in his attempt to have the participants explain the proceedings, Ishbel managed, with the aid of a contemporary publication on the West Coast Indians, to describe in some detail the significance as well as the nature of the ceremony.[76]

Yet Lady Aberdeen's approbation of Indian culture was far from total, for she was simultaneously attracted by romantic images and repelled by the harsh reality of 'miserable specimens in dirty squalid-coloured blankets [who] haunt the railway stations, with the object of selling buffalo horns, or baskets, or feather-work.'[77] More particularly, her concern at the anticipated extinction of an entire race was tempered by a blend of imperialism and evangelicalism which demanded the subjugation and conversion of the unregenerate, misguided red man. A romantic quality such as the Indians' 'wonderful and heroic endurance of pain' would become acceptable 'if it can only be made use of for the service of the God of love, and the betterment of their race, instead of for such purposes as the deliberate maiming and wounding of themselves in order to please the imaginary requirements of the Great Spirit.'[78] Although she certainly attributed the erosion of Indian civilization in part to the European avarice which had dispossessed the Indian of his ancestral lands, she saw no disparity between her lament for a race which would 'ere long disappear'and her praise of the 'predestined work' of missionaries and politicians to ensure the Indians' assimilation.[79] Even though she was uncomfortably aware that not all European values were to be admired or copied, Ishbel remained firmly convinced that the betterment of the Indians was dependent on their adoption of European values. She singled out Crowfoot, the late chief of the Blackfoot, for particular praise as 'one of the far-seeing Indians who understood that it was for the ultimate good of the country that the white men should take possession of the country, that railways should traverse its length and breadth, though bringing destruction to the Red Men's hunting-grounds, and that the land should be brought under the dominion of the plough.'[80] She seems to have been unaware of any contradiction between her criticism of European settlers for dispossessing the Indians of their hunting grounds and food supplies, and her own enjoyment of the 'splendid sport' available on the family's Okanagan Valley ranches. But Ishbel could not help being a child of her time, and her faith in the British imperial ideal permeated her attitude to Indians just as it permeated her one-sided interpretation of Quebec history, or her encouragement to domestic servants and small farmers to transfer their energies and loyalties to the wider Britain across the Atlantic.[81]

Conclusion

Through Canada with a Kodak is only one of many travelogues and guidebooks published in Britain in the late Victorian era which both stimulated and reflected contemporary interest in emigration, along with confident imperialist assumptions about Britain's relationship with her dominions. Lady Aberdeen's encouragement to 'the right sort of emigrant' was part and parcel of the prevailing national confidence in the political and economic future of the imperial relationship, in which the populating of Canada and the exploitation of its natural resources were to play a vital part. Like many guidebook writers, she was convinced that honesty, adaptability, and a determination to work hard were the only requirements for success, particularly in the developing West, and she emphasized these qualities repeatedly in her advice to farm labourers and – especially – domestic servants.

But the book is not simply a manual for emigrants. Lady Aberdeen, through the publication of her travel diary, was an active participant in the establishment of a thriving tourist industry in late nineteenth-century Canada, while at the same time demonstrating personally the characteristics of both the traditional traveller and the modern tourist. Although at times she displayed the tourist's readiness to follow an increasingly prescribed, packaged, and sanitized itinerary, on the whole she exemplified the open-minded, inquiring attitude of the genuine traveller in search of adventure, determined not to express unqualified approbation of disappointing sites like Niagara just because it was expected of her. Her independent outlook is reflected in the incisiveness of the narrative, with its refreshing lack of clichés or stereotypes, and the infectious excitement she demonstrated as the train carrying her westwards approached the Rockies, by the 1890s one of the few enduring symbols of the fast-retreating frontier.

The Aberdeens, of course, were not ordinary travellers; they were distinguished visitors, whose status gave them an immediate passport to the higher echelons of Canadian society. Yet their fame – which was to increase when Lord Aberdeen was appointed governor general only three years after their first visit – meant that they saw Canadian life from a different perspective than most travellers or emigrants, and in many ways *Through Canada with a Kodak* reflects the elevated political and social circles in which they moved. But the book is much more than a diary of society meetings; it is a lively and articulate presentation of an individual's first impressions of Canada, from Quebec to Vancouver, written by an enthusiastic Canadianist primarily for the edification of domestic servants, but subsequently made available to a wider readership in response to public demand. Canada is depicted not only in word, but also in picture, through the inclusion of both formal, professional photographs and casual snapshots taken with Ishbel's newly acquired Kodak camera. The result is an entertaining illustrated guide to late nineteenth-century Canada, which is valuable both in its own right and as a historical source, exemplifying the positive image of Canada held by tourists and emigrants alike, and cultivated in the fervent imperialist climate of late Victorian Britain. Even Dr Johnson might not have been too disappointed.[82]

NOTES

1 R.G. Moyles and D. Owram, *Imperial Dreams and Colonial Realities: British Views of Canada, 1880–1914* (Toronto, 1989), p. 116. For further details of agency activity, see H.G. Skilling, *Canadian Representation Abroad: From Agency to Embassy* (Toronto, 1945), and Marjory Harper, *Emigration from North East Scotland*, vol. 2, *Beyond the Broad Atlantic* (Aberdeen, 1988), ch. 1.
2 For a detailed assessment of the connection between the romantic movement and the development of tourism in Canada, see Patricia Jasen, 'Romanticism, Modernity and the Evolution of Tourism on the Niagara Frontier, 1790–1850,' *Canadian Historical Review* 73, no. 3 (Sept. 1991): 283–318.
3 Advertisement in the Advocates' Library copyright copy of *Through Canada with a Kodak*. I am indebted to John Morris, Assistant Keeper at the National Library of Scotland, Department of Printed Books, for this and all other information pertaining to W.H. White & Co. Ltd.
4 For further details of the Marjoribanks family, and Ishbel's childhood, see Doris French, *Ishbel and the Empire: A Biography of Lady Aberdeen* (Toronto and Oxford, 1988), pp. 16, 21–2.
5 The seventh Earl's grandfather, the fourth Earl, had served

as Foreign Secretary under Wellington and Peel, and as Conservative prime minister from 1852 to 1856.
6 See The Marquis and Marchioness of Aberdeen and Temair, *'We Twa': Reminiscences of Lord and Lady Aberdeen* vol. I, (London, 1926), pp. 174–7 for details of the rescue of the slaves and their subsequent experiences.
7 For discussion of the reasons underlying landlords' eviction of labourers (and tenant farmers), and the more benevolent policy followed on the Aberdeen estate, see Marjory Harper, *Emigration from North-East Scotland*, vol. 1, *Willing Exiles*, p. 158 and vol. 2, *Beyond the Broad Atlantic*, pp. 52 and 95, n. 3.
8 *Aberdeen Free Press*, 22 March 1883; and Ishbel, Marchioness of Aberdeen and Temair, *The Musings of a Scottish Granny* (London, 1936), p. 106.
9 *Mistresses and Maidservants: Suggestions towards the Increased Pleasure and Permanence of Their Domestic Relations* (Aberdeen, 1884).
10 By 1894 the association boasted 8,600 associates and members and 120 branches, including 2 in Canada. By 1897 two more branches had been formed in Canada. See the introduction to *Onward and Upward: Extracts (1891–1896) from the Magazine of the Onward and Upward Association*, selected and introduced by James Drummond (Aberdeen, 1983) and Alexander Gammie, 'The Countess of Aberdeen's Work for Women,' *Sunday Strand*, August 1906 (Haddo House MSS, pamphlet collection).
11 For further details of the Aberdeen Ladies' Union, and particularly its encouragement of emigration, see Harper, *Beyond the Broad Atlantic*, pp. 250–87.
12 See below, p. 58.

13 National Archives of Canada, The Journal of Lady Aberdeen (unpublished), MG 27, C-1352 1L 1B5. See also J.T. Saywell, ed., *The Canadian Journal of Lady Aberdeen, 1893–1898* (Toronto, 1960); Ishbel, Marchioness of Aberdeen and Temair, *The Musings of a Scottish Granny*; The Marquis and Marchioness of Aberdeen and Temair, *'We Twa,'* vols. 1 and 2; and *More Cracks with 'We Twa'* (London, 1929).

14 For further discussion of the growth of popular photography on both sides of the Atlantic, including details of the technical processes involved, see Colin Ford, ed., *The Story of Popular Photography* (London, 1989) and Lily Koltun, ed., *Private Realms of Light: Amateur Photography in Canada, 1839–1940* (Markham, Ont., 1984). See also Brian Coe and Mark Haworth-Booth, *A Guide to Early Photographic Processes* (London, 1983); Brian Coe and Paul Gates, *The Snapshot Photograph: The Rise of Popular Photography, 1888–1939* (London, 1977); Margaret F. Harker, *Victorian and Edwardian Photographs* (London, 1975); and Oliver Mathews, *Early Photographs and Early Photographers: A Survey in Dictionary Form* (London, 1973).

15 Brian Coe, 'The Rollfilm Revolution' in Ford, ed., *The Story of Popular Photography*, p. 62.

16 Anon, 'The Winnipeg Camera Club,' *The Great West Magazine* 13 (new series), no. 1 (Sept. 1898): 6.

17 Marjorie Pentland, *A Bonnie Fechter: The Life of Ishbel Marjoribanks, Marchioness of Aberdeen and Temair* (London, 1952), p. 88.

18 Ibid, p. 90.

19 The Hamilton yacht photograph is one of a number of professional views of Hamilton which appear in the Aberdeens' 1890–1 Canadian album, some of which are reproduced in

Notes to pages xxviii–xxx

Through Canada with a Kodak. The photograph of the University buildings in Toronto from which Lady Aberdeen's drawing is copied is entitled 'Queen's College, Toronto, Ont., c. 1870'. Additional information on Canadian professional photographs was supplied by Andrew Rodger, Documentary Art and Photography Department of the National Archives of Canada, and is included in a tabulated, annotated summary of the illustrations in the Annotated List of Illustrations.

20 The albums are entitled 'Canada 1890–91' and 'Kodak snaps by I.A. [Ishbel Aberdeen] at Guisachan.' One photograph – 'Canadian Dick and Bill at Dollis Hill, Willesden' (p. 81) – has been traced to a family album entitled '1891–92 (mostly London).'

21 For example, the pony pictured on page 181 of the book is looking towards the camera, whereas the photograph in the family album shows it looking away from the camera. Similarly, the photograph of the 'Empress of India' which appears in the book (p. 201) was taken just after the almost identical version which appears in the album, this being evident by the different position of the vessel in relation to the shore. Among the photographs considerably enhanced by the publisher were those which appear on pages 99, 157, 160, 162, 163, 187, and 191. On some occasions, the Kodak snaps did not come out at all, as was the case with the photographs of the Guisachan fruit and vegetable crop (p. 190); or photographs mentioned in the text were not reproduced in the book, as was the case with the *Parisian* at Quebec (p. 14):

22 See below, p. 209. The photograph from which the sketch on page 219 has been copied is also located in the holdings

of the National Archives of Canada, C-49476, accession 1972-327.
23 Pp. 25 and 146. The photographs of George MacKay, Admiral Hotham, and HMS *Warspite* may also have been obtained from professional photographers on the West Coast.
24 Dr Johnson, *The Idler*, no. 97, 23 Feb. 1760.
25 For detailed analysis of the structure of the travel narrative, and the way in which it has shaped public perceptions of the locations treated (particularly Eastern Australia), see Paul Carter, *The Road to Botany Bay: An Essay in Spatial History* (London, 1987). The quotation is taken from page xxii.
26 For example, having made some brief comments about Native people seen from the train in the vicinity of Calgary, she continued, 'But travellers who pass through these countries only by the railway can know nothing of the lives and customs of the true type of Indian' (below, p. 128).
27 See above, p. xxxiii and n. 25.
28 A substantial part of Lady Aberdeen's Canadian diary was published in J.T. Saywell, ed., *The Canadian Journal of Lady Aberdeen, 1893–1898* (Toronto, 1960), and her reflections on British Columbia in R.M. Middleton, ed., *The Journal of Lady Aberdeen: The Okanagan Valley in the Nineties* (Victoria, BC, 1986). The following survey, however, makes use of some hitherto unpublished material.
29 See Marjory Harper, 'Emigration and the Salvation Army,' *Bulletin of the Scottish Institute of Missionary Studies*, n.s., no. 3–4 (1985–7): 22–9. Lady Aberdeen confessed to harbouring a 'certain fear' of the Salvation Army, which deterred her from venturing into the steerage to talk to its recruits.
30 Unpublished journal, 13 Aug. 1890.

31 Ibid, 19 Aug. 1890.
32 See below, p. 5.
33 *British Parliamentary Papers, Report to the President of the Local Government Board by Andrew Doyle, Local Government Inspector, as to the Emigration of Pauper Children to Canada*, 1875 (PP 1875, LXIII).
34 For further discussion of the Home Children movement, see Harper, *Beyond the Broad Atlantic*, pp. 183–206; 'The Juvenile Immigrant: Halfway to Heaven, or Hell on Earth?' in Catherine Kerrigan, ed., *The Immigrant Experience* (Guelph, 1992); Gillian Wagner, *Children of the Empire* (London, 1982); Joy Parr, *Labouring Children* (London/Montreal, 1980); Phyllis Harrison, ed., *The Home Children* (Winnipeg, 1979).
35 Unpublished journal, 22 Aug. 1890.
36 See below, p. 13.
37 See below, pp. 14, 16, 17.
38 For further discussion of the discrepancy between image and reality in late nineteenth-century accounts of French Canada, see Moyles and Owram, *Imperial Dreams and Colonial Realities*, ch. 4.
39 Unpublished journal, 26 Aug. 1890.
40 Smith and his cousin, George Stephen, also from northeast Scotland, were the leading financial figures behind the CPR, and in 1885 Smith drove the last spike into the transcontinental railway at Craigellachie, British Columbia. From 1896 until his death in 1914 he was Canadian high commissioner in Britain, and in 1897 he was created Baron Strathcona and Mount Royal.
41 See above, pp. lxvi–lxxiii and below, pp. 202–42.
42 Unpublished journal, 1 Sept. 1890.
43 Quoted in Marjorie Pentland, *A Bonnie Fechter*, p. 88.

44 Unpublished journal, 7 Sept. 1890.
45 Jasen, 'Romanticism, Modernity and the Evolution of Tourism on the Niagara Frontier,' 305.
46 Sir Alexander, a native of Yorkshire who had emigrated to Canada as an infant, had crossed the Atlantic some forty times, despite being a bad sailor. During the voyage he had kept the Aberdeens liberally supplied with fresh provisions. (Unpublished journal, 13, 19 Aug. 1890).
47 For further details on Mowat, Allan, and Blake, see *Macmillan Dictionary of Canadian Biography* (Toronto, 1978).
48 See below, p. 94.
49 Unpublished journal, 1 Oct. 1890. Annie Macpherson had been offered an 800-acre farm in Manitoba, where, she told Lady Aberdeen, she was considering settling crofters from the Scottish Highlands. This plan did not subsequently materialize.
50 Ibid, 2 Oct. 1890.
51 Ibid.
52 See above, pp. lix–lx, lxii–lxvi, and below, 153–98.
53 Unpublished journal, 4 Oct. 1890.
54 Ibid, 7 Oct. 1890. See also below, pp. 107–8, for the edited and published version of these remarks.
55 For further details of the Aberdeen Association, see Harper, *Beyond the Broad Atlantic*, pp. 256–9.
56 There are numerous publications dealing with Highland life in the eighteenth and nineteenth centuries. One of the best expositions of the economic and social problems confronting the region is Eric Richards' two-volume *History of the Highland Clearances* (London, 1982 and 1985).
57 Marjorie Pentland, *A Bonnie Fechter*, p. 91. Evidence regarding the financing of the scheme is contained in the follow-

ing Scottish Record Office files: AF 51/28, 51/66, 51/190/ 4200/191, 51/210/1110[?]. I am grateful to Wayne Norton of Kamloops for drawing this discrepancy and these references to my attention.
58 Information about Mills supplied in a private communication from Wayne Norton. The Killarney illustrations appear to consist of one Kodak snap (p. 110), one professional photograph (p. 109), and one drawing, copied from another professional photograph mounted in the family album.
59 Contemporary discussion of the Killarney and Saltcoats schemes is found in *British Parliamentary Papers, Select Committee Report into Emigration from the Congested Districts* (PP 1889 (274) vol. 10; PP 1890 (354) vol. 12; PP 1890–91 (152) vol. 11). See also Stuart Macdonald, 'Crofter Colonisation in Canada 1886–1892: The Scottish Political Background,' *Northern Scotland* 7, no. 1 (1986): 47–59; and Kent Stuart, 'The Scottish Crofter Colony, Saltcoats, 1889–1904,' *Saskatchewan History* 24, no. 2 (Spring 1971): 41–50.
60 Saywell, *The Canadian Journal of Lady Aberdeen, 1893–1898*, 30 Oct. 1894.
61 Unpublished journal, 11 Oct. 1890.
62 John A. Eagle, *The Canadian Pacific Railway and the Development of Western Canada* (Kingston, 1989), p. 150.
63 Doris French suggests that Drummond may have been the father of Ishbel's youngest child, Archie, born in autumn 1884. (Doris French, *Ishbel and the Empire: A Biography of Lady Aberdeen* [Toronto, 1988], p. 69).
64 See title pages of unpublished journal ('Letters from Canada to H.D. and J.S. from I.A. 1890,' and 'Letters from Canada and the U.S.A. to H.D. and J.S. from I.A. 1891'). Sinclair, who became Liberal MP for Dumbartonshire in

1892, married Marjorie Gordon in 1904 and subsequently (as Lord Pentland) served as Secretary for Scotland.
65 Unpublished journal, 20 Sept., 11 Oct. 1890.
66 Ibid, 13 Oct. 1890.
67 Ibid, 14 Oct. 1890.
68 Her meeting with the Aberdeenshire immigrant at Banff, for instance, actually took place on the return journey, and the Aberdeens' activities in Vancouver, which in the book precede their visit to Victoria, in fact took place after they had been to the island.
69 Unpublished journal, 30 Sept. 1891.
70 Ibid, 14 Oct. 1890.
71 For further discussion of the Aberdeens' investments in British Columbia, see Marjory Harper, 'A Gullible Pioneer? Lord Aberdeen and the Development of Fruit Farming in the Okanagan Valley, 1891–1921,' *British Journal of Canadian Studies* 1, no. 2 (Dec. 1986): 256–81.
72 Much more detailed discussion of the conflicting stereotypes of Indians in European thought and literature is found in Ray Allan Billington, *Land of Savagery/Land of Promise: The European Image of the American Frontier in the Nineteenth Century* (New York and London, 1981). Consideration of these issues with particular reference to female travellers and settlers is given in Sandra L. Myres, *Westering Women and the Frontier Experience, 1800–1915* (Albuquerque, 1982), ch. 3.
73 See, for example, 'The Last Home of the Red Man' (*Chambers' Journal*, 18 Feb. 1871), 'Indian Life in the Far West' (ibid, 27 July 1889), and 'Reminiscences among the Sioux Indians' (ibid, 6 Sept. 1890).
74 See below, p. 204.

75 See below, pp. 223–41. See also unpublished journal, 1 Oct. 1891. For an alternative descriptive of a potlatch ceremony, see 'An American Indian Potlatch' in *Chambers' Journal*, 13 April 1889, pp. 239–40.
76 Albert P. Niblack, *The Coast Indians of Southern Alaska and Northern British Columbia* (Washington, 1890).
77 See below, p. 128.
78 Ibid, pp. 218, 222.
79 Ibid, pp. 128, 130.
80 Ibid, p. 212.
81 For further discussion of these issues, see Moyles and Owram, *Imperial Dreams and Colonial Realities*, particularly ch. 7 for British writings on the Canadian Indian.
82 See above, p. xxxii.

THROUGH CANADA
WITH A KODAK

A Group of Canadian Boys photographed during a halt at a wayside station.

Through Canada

with a Kodak.

BY THE COUNTESS OF
ABERDEEN.

WITH ILLUSTRATIONS.

EDINBURGH:
W H. WHITE & CO.
1893.

THE great majority of the illustrations in this book are printed from photographs taken by Lady Aberdeen's Kodak; but in some instances use has been made of photographs collected by Lord and Lady Aberdeen when travelling. As these were, however, mostly unmounted, the name of the photographer does not always appear, so that acknowledgment of their origin cannot in every case be recorded. But special mention must be made of Messrs Notman of Montreal, and Messrs Boorne and May of Calgary, whose well known work will be recognised in some of the illustrations inserted.

If in some cases there is an unavoidable omission of acknowledgment, an apology is hereby offered, any such omission being quite unintentional.

PREFATORY NOTE.

THE papers contained in this little book were written during two tours in Canada, for the information and amusement of the Members and Associates of the ONWARD AND UPWARD ASSOCIATION, and were accordingly published in the Magazine *Onward and Upward* in 1891-92. They are merely the passing and superficial notes of a traveller journeying rapidly through the country, and desirous of conveying some impressions of the rich and varied attractions presented by "the Dominion," and which appear to be but very imperfectly realised by those at home, whether by the holiday seeker or the intending settler. They do not aspire to deal with the deeper questions of Canadian life or politics, but are merely recollections of delightful holiday trips made charming not only by the beauties of nature, but by the extraordinary kindness and hospitality of people of all classes in Canada. Looked upon thus in the light of a journal, these pages possess a peculiar attraction for their writer, in company with the little scraps of sketches and photographic views so dear to the heart of the tourist. But they appear to her to be scarcely worthy of being thus collected in the form of a volume. As, however, both the publisher and many kind readers of these jottings in their previous form have desired to see them thus gathered together, their wishes have been deferred to, and, with a full consciousness of their deficiencies, they are now gratefully dedicated to both the Members and Associates of the ONWARD AND UPWARD ASSOCIATION and to our friends and hosts in Canada.

ISHBEL ABERDEEN.

Haddo House, Aberdeenshire, April 1893

CONTENTS.

		PAGE
I.	OUTWARD BOUND,	1
II.	QUEBEC,	11
III.	MONTREAL,	23
IV.	A CANADIAN LAKE VOYAGE,	36
V.	HAMILTON,	43
VI.	TORONTO,	61
VII.	OTTAWA,	71
VIII.	ACROSS THE PRAIRIES,	91
IX.	IN A RAILWAY ACCIDENT,	113
X.	THE ROCKY MOUNTAINS,	131
XI.	A VISIT TO BRITISH COLUMBIA,	153
XII.	GUISACHAN FARM,	169
XIII.	THE INDIANS OF CANADA,	197
XIV.	MORE ABOUT THE INDIANS AND THEIR CUSTOMS,	212
XV.	MANNERS AND TRADITIONS OF THE INDIANS OF THE COAST AND ISLANDS,	223
	APPENDIX,	243

LIST OF ILLUSTRATIONS.

Group of Canadian Boys,	*Frontispiece*
Outward Bound,	2
A Last Peep of "Ould Ireland." *From a Sketch by* LADY ABERDEEN,	3
The First Iceberg on the Horizon. *From a Sketch by* LADY ABERDEEN,	8
Quebec, from the South Side of the River,	10
Quebec, from Montmorenci. *From a Sketch by* LADY ABERDEEN,	15
The Falls of Montmorenci,	18
A Quebec Calèche,	21
Jacques Cartier,	24
Montreal,	25
Sir Donald Smith,	29
Father Lacombe,	31
"The First Communion." *From a Photo of Picture by Jules Breton, in the possession of Sir Donald Smith*,	35
Kingston, Ontario. *From a Sketch by* LADY ABERDEEN,	39
Highfield, Hamilton, Ontario,	45
The Gore, Hamilton, Ontario,	47
Lord Haddo and Lady Marjorie H. Gordon,	49
Hon. Dudley and Hon. Archie H. Gordon,	50
A Hamilton Yacht,	51

List of Illustrations.

	PAGE
View on Hamilton Bay,	55
The Lads and Lassies who accompanied us,	59
University Buildings, Toronto,	63
Captain Macmaster,	66
Government House, Toronto,	67
The late Sir Alexander Campbell,	68
Falls of Niagara,	73
Above Niagara,	74
View of Ottawa,	75
Lord Stanley (now Earl of Derby),	76
Lady Stanley (now Countess of Derby),	77
Sir John Abbott,	79
A pair of Acadian or Sand Whet Owls,	80
Canadian "Dick" and "Bill" at Dollis Hill, Willesden,	81
The View from the Terrace outside Parliament Buildings,	84
Rideau Hall, Ottawa,	87
The Toboggan Slide at Rideau Hall,	89
Westward!	90
All Aboard!	92
The Car in which we travelled West,	93
John Barber, our Car Porter,	95
A Young Settlement,	96
Mr and Mrs O'Brien,	98
All that is left of the Buffalo,	99
How a journey from Winnipeg for Ottawa was accomplished in days gone by,	101
Manitou, Manitoba,	104
Greetings from a Group of Manitobans,	106
Mr and Mrs Peter Graham's Cottage,	109
Mr and Mrs John Campbell's House,	110
The Darough Family at Glenfern,	111
Scene of Accident. *From a Sketch by* LADY ABERDEEN,	115
Our Engine, as Photographed after the Accident,	116
Off Again!	117
A Regiment of Workers on the Prairie,	122
One of Sir John Lister-Kaye's big Farms in Alberta,	124
Passing a Car-full of Emigrants—"Take our Pictures,"	125
Map showing region of Summer droughts in North America,	126
A Horse Ranch near Calgary,	127
Approaching the Rockies,	132
"The Three Sisters,"	133
View from the Window of the Banff Hotel,	135
Cascade Mountain, Banff,	136
The Van Horne Range, sketched from Field by LADY ABERDEEN,	139
A Trestle Bridge,	140

List of Illustrations.

	PAGE
Vancouver,	142
The late Mr G. G. Mackay,	143
Lieut-Governor of British Columbia,	146
Admiral Hotham,	147
H.M.S. "Warspite,"	148
Lord Aberdeen and Prof. H. Drummond in the Railway Car,	151
The first Passenger Train on the Shushwap and Okanagan Line,	157
Mr Lequime's little Steamer,	159
Transferring the Luggage from the Train to the Steamer,	160
Entrance Gate to Guisachan Farm,	162
In the Woods of Guisachan, B. C.,	163
View from the front-door of Guisachan. *From a sketch by* LADY ABERDEEN,	165
Guisachan, B. C.,	166
Going out for a Bear Hunt,	170
Watching the Game-bag,	171
"Foo," our Chinese Cook,	172
Willy, the Indian boy, with his white pony	173
Residence No. 1,	174
Residence No. 2,	175
Residence No. 3,	176
Residence No. 4,	177
The Guisachan Staff,	179
Starting for a Drive with "Charlie" and "Pinto,"	180
Mr Smith exhibiting the wild Indian pony,	181
Coutts on "Aleck"—"Spot" in attendance,	183
Planting Scotch Firs from Guisachan, Inverness-shire, at Guisachan, B. C.,	187
S.S. "Penticton" waiting to bear us away,	191
Good bye!	193
Going to work at Coldstream Ranch,	199
The s.s. "Empress of India,"	201
Sarcee Indians,	209
Crowfoot, Chief of the Blackfeet,	213
Indian curios. *Drawn by* Mr J. GRANT,	214, 215, 216, 217, 225, 226, 227, 228, 229, 231, 232, 233, 234, 235, 237, 239, 241.
Making a "Brave" at the Sun-dance,	219
An Indian Lodge or Wigwam,	221
Eastern part of Kasa-an Village, Prince of Wales' Island, Alaska,	224
Memorial bust of Sir John Macdonald,	245
Homeward bound,	249

I.

OUTWARD BOUND.

A TRIP to Canada! Yes, we had often talked about it. We had paid a visit to India, Ceylon, Australia, Tasmania, New Zealand; and we much wished to see something of this other vast and fair Dominion, which forms part of the British Empire. But, in spite of our voyagings, we have never been friends of the sea; and when we talked of Canada we were always very conscious of the fact that the wild waves of the ocean separated its shores by the space of seven days from Britain.

However, last year our desires, coupled with doctor's advice, overcame our fears, and on a fine evening in August we found ourselves dropping down the Mersey on board the s.s. "Parisian" of the Allan Line, one of the largest ships plying between this country and Canadian ports. Have you ever been on board an Atlantic liner when in port? If so, you know how delightful everything looks. A large beautiful deck above, snug little berths below; a splendid saloon, a reading-room, a smoking-room, books, music, games;

and you look in the pretty little prospectuses handed to you about the interior arrangements of the ship, and you see pictures of a happy company seated at long tables enjoying the best of fare, ladies and gentlemen

Outward Bound—The "Parisian" "dropping down the Mersey."

singing and playing, reading, and playing at games, and altogether having a good time of it. Look at the pictures given in those pages, and say whether life at sea does not seem a very attractive thing, sailing along in one of these brave ships under a good captain, surrounded by luxuries, and with no cares, no responsibilities, no work, no telegrams, no letters?

So one thinks, and so one continues to think for an hour or two after starting; but wait a wee, and see if you don't begin to wish that you could give effect to second thoughts, when you find yourself tossing about in the Irish Channel in a gale a few hours later. But the least said

A last peep of "Ould Ireland.

about these experiences, and the wishes then rashly uttered, the better; and so I will tell you nothing of that August night, nor of the long wait we had next day at Moville, near Londonderry, for the English mails, which had been delayed some hours in crossing from Holyhead to Kingstown, in consequence of the storm. I should like, though, to be able to give you a sight of our last glimpse of the shores of "Ould Ireland," as we saw them disappearing next evening. A succession of bold bluffs and headlands jutting out into the sea, one beyond the other, as far as the eye could reach in the gathering darkness, the green slopes here and there just visible, and the heavy black clouds which had been overhanging us all day fringed with a glory of red and purple and orange. Lord Aberdeen and I leant over the taff-rail and caught some whiffs of a dear familiar peat-smoke, which sent us happy to our cabins that night Pray enquire no further: you shall hear none of our groans. Suffice it to say that the 750 passengers on board were in a decidedly subdued frame of mind for a few days, your Editor amongst the number. She had not yet even conceived the idea of telling her friends of the Onward and Upward Association something about this expedition, or else she would doutbless have used her Kodak, to bring before you various scenes and attitudes of different degrees of misery. Our fellow-passengers therefore escaped the danger of being introduced thus to you, and I shall hope to show some of them to you in a happier aspect later on. When we began to be in a state to realise one another, we found that we might almost consider ourselves already in Canada. We were of all degrees: cabinet ministers, governors, senators, professors, business men, were there, and so were also emigrants of many various classes and from all countries, bound to many various destinations.

Some were going for the first time to seek their fortune, they knew not where; some were going out to join friends who had already prospered; some were returning from paying a brief visit to their friends in "the old country," as we soon became Canadian enough to call it. Amongst such company, who were all also so willing to impart information to strangers and "tenderfeet" (this being the name for new-comers in Canada), we were able to pick up a good deal about the country and the people amongst whom we were going to live for the next three months. I will try to filter down to you a little of what they told us by degrees, but first I want to introduce to you a number of youthful emigrants, in whom I think you will be specially interested. These are a party of fifty young girls of all ages, from three to seventeen, taken from misery and destitution to Miss Rye's Homes, from whence they will be drafted, either as servants or else adopted into colonists' homes. Much care has to be used in selecting only suitable, healthy children for emigration, but when this care is used there are endless openings for them in Canada. Miss Macpherson, whose name is so well known as having been the first lady to undertake the emigration of children, told us that this year she had had 900 applications for children, of which she had only been able to supply 150.

These little ones whom we saw on board the "Parisian" were all full of eager expectation regarding their new homes, and, after the first few days of sea-sickness and discomfort consequent on the vaccination to which every steerage passenger to Canada must submit, they made themselves very happy with their skipping-ropes and various games. A part of the ship had been partitioned off and fitted up on purpose for them—a little dining place, a row of little tin basins and two storeys of little box-like berths where they lay snugly packed away at night; the kind matron, who had crossed the ocean some forty times on like business, sleeping in a little cabin opening into this special section.

The chaplain accompanying the ship often had special services for the children, and it was very pleasant to hear the bright hymn-singing, which always brought together a number of the other passengers. As we think of those little ones we wonder how they are getting on in their scattered homes. We had hoped to see them again in Miss Rye's Home, near Niagara, but, to our regret, we never managed the expedition. The matron told us that very probably a fortnight after we landed the children would all be engaged, or adopted in homes where they knew they would be cared for. I think I have behaved very badly to you in not having photographed either these children for you, or a typical emigrant Norwegian family, who would have made a delightful group if I could have made them understand what I wanted. There they were, father, mother, and a whole succession of little flaxen-haired boys and girls, the latter each with a little yellow pig-tail, after the fashion of some of the foreign dolls we buy. There are always a number of Scandinavians in every ship-load of emigrants going to Canada, for they are most thrifty, hard-working people, and when they get settled, generally soon send money home to bring out their relations. I shall have more to tell you about them by-and-by. Meantime, I must tell you about what is always the great excitement of a voyage to Canada. We were seven days out from Liverpool, and were preparing, in various ways, for a concert, which was to be given on behalf of the Liverpool Home for the Orphan Children of Seamen who have perished at sea, when a rumour went round that an iceberg was in sight. An eager crowd was soon scanning the horizon with telescopes and field-glasses, and before long a tiny, cone-shaped, glistening white hill hove in sight, resplendent with shades of transparent green and blue. We looked at it, and we photographed it, and we sketched it, and we talked about it, till another, and yet another, came in view, and during that evening and next day some thirteen were seen in all the various lights of sunset and sunrise, and mid-day They were very beautiful, but their beauty needs to be *seen* to be understood. I am almost ashamed to let you see the reproduction of a little sketch I attempted when the first iceberg was visible on the horizon. These icebergs, which are morsels detached from the great glaciers of Greenland by the summer sun, cause great anxiety to the officers commanding ships on the Atlantic. This is more especially the case in the neighbourhood of Newfoundland, which is very subject to fogs; for, as the saying goes, it is celebrated for "fog, dog, and cod." Often and often ships have to lie outside the Straits of Belle-Isle for days enwrapped in dense fog, afraid to budge,

The first Iceberg on the Horizon

in case one of these great ice monsters may be looming near at hand, ready to overwhelm the unwary seaman and his craft. This very ship of ours, the "Parisian," had a narrow escape in May. In the fog she ran atilt against what was called a small iceberg, but which one of the passengers decribed to me as having a most alarming appearance. In a moment there appeared as a vision just in front of the bows, a towering white mass, part of which seemed to overshadow the deck.

This passenger told me that the feeling of alarm was swallowed up in an overpowering sense of wonder and awe at the marvellousness and magnificence of the scene presented, and that it was only later, when the skill of captain and officers had averted a catastrophe, that the perilous position in which the ship had been placed was fully realised.

The bright sun and clear skies which we enjoyed gave us immunity from all such dangers. We sailed peacefully through the Straits, on either side of us the line of the low blue hills of Labrador and Newfoundland gleaming in the sun, and in the reflected light of long, trailing, flaky, pinky-white clouds, which we soon began to associate with Canadian skies. Then we floated out of sight of land again, into the great Gulf of St Lawrence, on into the big river itself, along the picturesque shores of French Canada, dotted with groups of cosy, wee, tin-roofed cottages, in which lived the French-Canadian fishermen, and every now and again a picturesque little church and school. It was all very peaceful, and a great contrast to the beginning of our voyage. But I must not linger longer over our voyage, and so I leave you, till next letter, within sight of the beautiful city of Quebec.

Quebec, from the South Side of the River.

II.

QUEBEC.

NO words could ever describe Quebec; so you must try to form an idea of it from the pictures we have given you. We saw it in every variety of weather :—first, in the uncertain reddish light of a dull sunrise on the morning of our arrival; and next in a howling storm; then, when its bright spires glittered in the glorious Canadian noon-day, or with the grey of its old gables transfigured in the sunset. We saw its bright roofs and spires bathed in the sunlight of noon; again in all the glories of a gold and purple sunset; and at night we saw the whole city gleaming with the myriads of electric lights shining about her crags. Quebec exercises a curious fascination on the visitor; it transports him into the past whether he wills it or no; the sentiment of the place dominates him, and it is the only town that I have seen which I can conceive imposing on her children the same strange potent spell which binds us Scotch folk to our own never-to-be-surpassed "Auld Reekie."

It is strange that the emigrant to the New World

should make acquaintance with it first in this old-world city, full of associations and traces of the past—its very inhabitants seeming to transport you to a France of two or three centuries ago. Nevertheless the emigrant will find that the demands of the present and future have not been forgotten, that his needs have not been overlooked, and that the Government and the Railway Companies have amply provided for his reception. And besides the Government and the Railways, there is the Women's Protective Immigration Society, which takes special charge of all women emigrants disembarking at Quebec, whether travelling alone, or with one of those protected parties—by far the best auspices to travel under—which have special arrangements on board ship, and a matron to themselves. I hope to say something later on in these papers to young women thinking of emigrating; but meanwhile I would like to take this opportunity of saying that there is a constant demand for women-servants in all parts of Canada, the wages being from $8 to $12 (£1, 12s. to £2, 8s.) a month in Eastern Canada, and increasing as you go Westward to as much as $20 (£4) per month. Good general servants, who are not afraid to work, and who will adapt themselves to the ways of the country, are sure to get on in Canada and to find happy homes. Girls who only wish to take to one branch of domestic work had better not go, except in limited numbers, as it is the exception, not the rule, to keep more than one servant, and those will succeed best who will put their hands heartily and readily to anything. Servants who have had some training in general work will be particularly valued. If any girls reading these words make up their minds to emigrate, they cannot do better than go out with one of the protected parties arranged by the Hon. Mrs Joyce, of the United British Women's Emigration Society. The passage with one of these parties costs £4, 10s., and all who go may be sure of securing a situation immediately on arrival.

But to return to our own doings at Quebec. The scene on our arrival at the wharf was a busy one. Most of the emigrants disembarked here, and we saw our little friends destined for Miss Rye's Homes marched off two and two very happily to the train which was to convey them further West. There were a great many "Good-byes" to be said to our good captain and officers, and to the friends we had made on our passage out, and who were all now dispersing far and near. Soon we were crossing the river in a ferry-boat, and next found ourselves dashing up the queerest, quaintest, roughest, steepest streets you can imagine. These led up to the Citadel, which crowns the heights, and where the Governor-General lives when he is staying at Quebec.

The present Governor-General, Lord Stanley of Preston, and his wife, Lady Stanley, were not at Quebec when we arrived; but they sent us the kindest of welcomes, along with a hospitable invitation to stay at the Citadel. And never did any guests feel more grateful than we, when we found ourselves in a cosy room overlooking the town and the busy river. We watched our old friend the "Parisian" making ready for her further journey to Montreal, and we "Kodaked" her, and, as she steamed away, waved our final greetings with a towel out of the window.

Then we had time to take in our position, and to survey the whole surrounding country from a delightful terrace which had been built out beyond the spacious ball-room erected whilst Lord Lorne and Princess Louise were in Canada. In the distance lay long lines of low blue hills; the broad, stately river winding below, laden with vessels of every description bound to and from many European ports, while darting in and out amongst them flashed the white sails of pleasure boats. The city, with the imposing tower of its University, its many spires, its bright roofs made of plates of tin, presents a strange contrast to the heights clad with verdure and forest which met the eye of the adventurous French explorer, Jacques Cartier, who arrived here in the autumn of 1535, with his three ships, the "Grande Hermine" (120 tons), the "Petite Hermine" (60 tons), and the "Emerillon' (40 tons), and stayed one whole winter. We could not but often dream that we could see those three brave little ships, with their gallant captain, floating in these

Quebec, from Montmorenci.

unexplored waters, and exciting the wonder of the Indian Prince Donnacona and his savages, crowding around the new arrivals in their little bark canoes.

You must get out your history-books if you want to go back to that time, and, if you want to trace out how Quebec was founded a half-century later by Champlain, how it became half a mission, half a trading station, how it was defended against the many attacks of the Indians and became the centre of the Colony of New France; and then how it was neglected and misgoverned by corrupt officials from France, and finally how it was conquered by the splendid daring of General Wolfe in 1759. We had the great advantage of seeing the scenes of all these historic deeds under the able guidance of M. Lemoine, the historian of Quebec, to whose kind care we had been confided by our friend Sir Alexander Campbell, Lieutenant-Governor of Ontario, whom we were fortunate enough to have as one of our fellow-passengers in the "Parisian." M. Lemoine showed us the steep precipitous cliff up which Wolfe and his men clambered that memorable night, and the spot where he overthrew the few men carelessly guarding the heights: where his men formed up in line, and advanced over the plains of Abraham: where Montcalm, the gallant French defender, rode out and saw the English red-coats, and heard the Highland bagpipes, and exclaimed, "This is a serious business!" Then we saw the spot where Wolfe fell pierced by three bullets—where he fell, only to hear the cry, a moment later, "They run! see how they run!" "Who run?" demanded Wolfe. "The enemy, sir. They give way everywhere." "Go," said the dying man, "go, one of you to Colonel Burton, and tell him to march Webb's regiment down to Charles River, to cut off their retreat from the bridge." And then, turning on his side he murmured, "Now God be praised. I will die in peace," and expired. Almost at the same moment his noble-hearted enemy received his death-wound, though riding into the city he tried to reassure his friends, saying "It is nothing; it is nothing!" We saw also the monument in the Governor's garden, which commemorates both the conquered and the conquering General.

But I have not space to tell more of all we saw at Quebec, nor of the delightful day we spent at the falls of Montmorenci—higher than those of Niagara—and known to the people of the neighbourhood as "La Vache" (the cow), because the foam has the appearance of frothing milk.

In the winter this spray freezes till a cone is formed some seventy feet high. Then sledges with metal runners called "*toboggans*" are prepared, and from the height of this cone the young people of Quebec amuse themselves by shooting down one after another, and sliding away far across the smooth surface of the river below. Oh, the fun these Canadians have in winter,

The Falls of Montmorenci.

with their sledging, their skating, their tobogganing, and their snow-shoe expeditions. The snow-shoe is a necessary equipment for those who have to take long journeys in the winter. It looks rather like a lawn-tennis racket, and consists of a light frame with netting across, which prevents the wearer from sinking into the snow. But some practice is required in order to use this novel oot-gear easily.

One word about the French Canadians. They are a thrifty, contented, law-abiding, religious people. When the British conquered Quebec they wisely allowed the people to retain their own laws and customs, and the result is that nowhere can be found more loyal subjects of the British Crown. The atmosphere of modern France has never reached them, and they are still the same simple Norman and Briton peasants who came out some hundreds of years ago. They are very much influenced by their priests, who maintain a strict rule over them and all their family affairs. The regulations are very strict—for instance, about dancing, the popular snow-shoe expeditions, and other amusements. Some restrictions are, however, being relaxed. For example, fifty years ago meat was absolutely forbidden all through the forty days of Lent, and this was found to be a great hardship in many cases in that severe climate. The rule has not been so rigidly enforced of late years.

The French in Canada are increasing rapidly by reason

of the large families they generally have. Twelve, fourteen, and sixteen children are quite an ordinary-sized family, while we heard of a well-authenticated case of one couple rearing forty-four children. The country is therefore filling up, and some of the people are moving into the New England States, and westward to Manitoba.

The general desire is, however, to stick to their own country, and the Quebec Government facilitates this by giving 100 acres free to every family which numbers twelve children. As we drove along the well-kept road to and from Montmorenci, we passed various characteristic little villages; the houses bear evidence of being built for contingencies of either extremes of climate: verandahs and green sun-shutters, and netting over doors and windows, as protection against the blazing heat and the mosquitoes and flies, but also peculiarly-shaped roofs, curved at the bottom in such a way as to prevent the snow from making a permanent lodgment.

The crops we saw were very poor indeed, but we were told that it had been a very bad year for agriculturists round about Quebec. We were especially struck by the universal civility and gentle courtesy of the people—no pushing either of themselves or of their sights, only a quiet readiness to help strangers, and to give them any information which they might be in need of, without looking for reward. When we were in Quebec we imagined this was the hereditary French politeness showing itself, but our experience afterwards showed us that civility and a spirit of kindliness towards visitors is more or less a characteristic of all Canadians.

There is much more that I would like to tell you about Quebec and its neighbourhood, but my space is more than filled, and I cannot even describe to you the little carts, dragged by dogs trained to harness, like those

A Quebec Calèche.

used in this country in bygone days, until they were forbidden by law; nor yet can I dilate on the curious old-fashioned vehicle, peculiar to Quebec, called a *calèche*. You see a picture of one here. Try to imagine a very high gig, with a hood, swung on enormously high C-shaped springs; next imagine a weedy-looking horse tearing along, after the fashion of Quebec horses, at full gallop up and down streets steeper than the Edinburgh High Street, and full of holes and pitfalls, and then you will be able to judge of the courage of those who trust their persons in such a conveyance. Nevertheless, I will confide to you that we found this method of progression most comfortable, and we congratulate Quebecers on having discovered a way of making the roughness of their streets unperceivable to the traveller.

And now adieu to Quebec. We shall meet again in Montreal.

III.

MONTREAL.

"GLAD to see you at Montreal!" "Well, and what do you think of Canada?" "Lord Aberdeen, I think? You're heartily welcome, sir!" "Grand hotel this! Nothing to beat it on the Continent!" Such-like were the greetings which fell on our ears as we entered into the vast central hall of the Windsor Hotel, Montreal, after a hot and dusty railway journey from Quebec. This hall and the spacious dining-saloon and public drawing-rooms of the hotel are practically a club for the inhabitants of Montreal and its visitors. Here we find many of our fellow-passengers from the "Parisian" again—here, too, was our captain; this celebrity and that were pointed out to us by the head waiter, as they sat at the innumerable small tables at meals, and before many hours had passed we felt ourselves quite *habitués* of Canada's commercial capital, and accustomed to her ways. Quite conscientiously, too, could we pass muster with the most exacting Canadian in paying due tribute to the comforts, the conveniences, and the splendour of the Windsor Hotel.

As at Quebec, our thoughts irresistibly turned to the contrast between this proud and splendid city, with her beautiful buildings, and churches, and universities, to the nestling Indian village found by Jacques Cartier at

Jacques Cartier.

the foot of the mountain which he first called Mont Royal (the royal mountain), in honour of his king. We fancied we could see the groups of "braves," with their squaws and children, crowding out of their little huts to

Montreal.

look at these strange beings; the women stroking the moustaches and beards of the explorers, to make sure of their reality; the infirm, and sick, and feeble, with their paralysed chief at their head, imploring for the "healing touch" which they believed these denizens of another world could give.

The words which were spoken by Maisonneuve, the leader of the little band of forty-five emigrants who landed on the island of Montreal in 1642, with the intention of founding a colony and a mission, have indeed come true. No sooner had the little party landed than they gathered together for prayer and in consecration of their mission in this new land, and at the close of their worship Maisonneuve turned to his companions and said, "You are a grain of mustard seed that shall rise and grow till its branches overshadow the earth. You are few, but your work is the work of God. His smile is on you, and your children shall fill the land."

Many were the vicissitudes which that little colony had to pass through, many were the heroes and heroines whom they were destined to nurture amidst the rough experiences of a life spent in constant dread and danger of the Indian's tomahawk and scalping-knife. But Maisonneuve's words proved prophetic, and in place of the small barricaded fort of Villa Marie of Montreal, defended by a few missionaries and devoted women, there rears itself the largest, most prosperous city in

Canada, sheltered by her Royal Mountain, on which she lavishes her proud care. A lovely winding drive has been laid out round the sides of the mountain, by which the visitor gradually ascends to a standpoint, from which a glorious view of the river and scenery below must be obtained.

Unfortunately the weather was very unfavourable when we made the ascent, and we could only form a dim conception of the splendid panorama spread out before us, with the rushing white waters of the Lachine Rapids in the distance. But you can get an idea of the view from the picture we have given you.

On the sides of the mountain itself large and most carefully-tended cemeteries have been laid out separately for Protestants and Roman Catholics, and are considered one of the sights of the place. We drove through them, admiring many strange bright plants and trees, and then we wended our way to return a visit made to us in the morning by an old friend of the family, Mr Crombie, who had been for many years a London City Missionary, but who has now in his old age gone out with his wife to make his home with his son, a minister in charge of a Presbyterian Church in Montreal. We found them enthusiastic in praise of their new country, and the beneficial effects that its climate had had on their health.

But I must cry, Halt! For I see that I am dangerously

near writing a journal of all our doings, and this will never do. So, only one or two more remarks about Montreal, where, indeed, we only stayed two nights, as we were hurrying on to our children, who had preceded us across the ocean. But we had time to inspect a pleasant little Home for Female Emigrants in Mansfield Street, which is under the charge of a lady who takes the liveliest interest in those who pass through her hands. They are met at the steamers, and for the first twenty-four hours can remain at the Home free of all charge. Very often, even on the first day, they find places to which they can go at once, but if they require to stay a little longer they pay a small sum per day. But all may be sure of a welcome here, and of help and wise advice.

And then I must tell you of the evening we spent at the beautiful house of Sir Donald Smith, whose name is a household word in Canada, as well it may be, for he has acted the part of a fairy godfather to his adopted country. I think we must some day try if Sir Donald cannot be persuaded to tell the O.U.A. some of his stories of the by-gone days of the Hudson's Bay Company, of which he is President, and in whose service he has taken many an adventurous journey. He could tell us not only of the hardships of cold, but of the hardships of heat, which beset the hunter. That very evening we were with him he told us of the terrors of the Labrador mosquitoes, and how they have vanquished men who

Sir Donald Smith.

would fly from no other enemy. He instanced one case in which a friend of his was so sensitive to their bites, that he had to stop every half-hour on the march to wash away the blood which was pouring from his head and face.

We had all manner of stories that night, for amongst Sir Donald's guests were—Mr Shaughnessy, the Vice-President of the Canadian Pacific Railway; the Rev· Mr Barclay, whom many of you may have heard of, as he was colleague with Dr Macgregor, at St Cuthbert's, Edinburgh, for some years before going to the Montreal congregation, by whom he is held in such high esteem; and last, but not least, Father Lacombe, a priest missionary amongst the Indians, who has given all his life to their cause. I have had a photograph of him engraved so that you may have a glimpse of the kindly, noble old face. He lives far away in the North-West, and is not often seen in civilised haunts, but his name is everywhere loved and respected among Protestants and Roman Catholics alike. His life of love and whole-hearted devotioin to his mission has gained for him enormous influence amongst *"mes sauvages,"* as he playfully calls the Indians. For instance, when the Canadian Pacific Railway Company first began to lay out their railway through the red man's territory, there were rumours, and more than rumours, that the wild "Bloods" and "Blackfeet" meditated wrecking the pathway of the

Father Lacombe.

iron fiend which threatened their solitudes. Father Lacombe's aid was invoked as mediator, and the "Bloods" and the "Blackfeet" buried the hatchet. His talk with us will always be a happy remembrance; his fatherly solicitude over his flock, and the way in which he identifies himself with them is most touching. "You must never drive the Indians, or frighten them; you must draw them by ever telling them of the love of the Father." Only once, he told us, was he in momentary danger from any Indian. An Indian lad had been falling into bad ways, and Father Lacombe told him that if he persisted in these ways he would surely reap the fruits of his sin. A few days later the boy was ill, and Father Lacombe went to see him, and, laying his hand on his knee, asked him how he was. The boy jumped up in a fury, and seizing a knife, made a lunge at the missionary, which, fortunately, the latter eluded by a rapid movement. The boy had remembered the words spoken to him a few days before, and thought that Father Lacombe had the power to bring punishment and death upon him by merely touching him. Amongst other work done for the Indian by this good man has been the making of grammars and translations of parts of the Bible, and other books for their use. He says that when he is quite worn out with active work, he will come and build a Hermitage near Haddo House, and write books for and about his Indians.

Some day I must tell you of other missions amongst the Indians, of the Church of England's Mission, and of our Presbyterian Church Mission, which are doing splendid work, and for which I would like to ask your support. To-day I have simply told you our impressions of one who is surely following Christ, if ever man did, and taking His message of love and mercy to dark souls, and to whom, therefore, all Christians can with heart and soul say, "God speed." Meanwhile I must tell you how Mr Barclay joined with Père Lacombe in telling us of the North-West. He had gone with the Canadian troops as chaplain, on the expedition to quell the last insurrection amongst the half-breeds, and we were told on all hands how magnificent his tall manly figure looked in uniform, and how his conduct with the troops won for him universal respect. I wish you could have heard him describing the services he had in far out-of-the-way places on the Sabbaths. The military band led the psalms and hymns, and the host of men's voices rose up in the open air, in regions where divine worship had never before awakened echoes, and amongst the worshippers were found lonely settlers who had for years been far from any church, and who hailed this opportunity of joining in public prayer and praise once more, and to whose eyes the sound of the well-known tunes brought tears of joy.

One more glimpse must I give you of the interior of

Sir Donald's hospitable mansion—not of his library, lined with the beautiful red wood of California and British Columbia; not of his unique Japanese room, where you might spend hours in examining curiosities which can be seen nowhere else out of Japan; not of his beautifully decorated drawing-rooms; but of one picture in his picture gallery. It is full of other treasures, but this is the one you would most like to see. It is painted by a French artist, and the scene is in France. A number of peasant girls, their heads veiled, after foreign custom, are passing up the lane to the little church in the distance, their friends standing about in groups invoking blessings on the young lives about to dedicate themselves to God's service. In the foreground of the picture we have a touching scene of one family kissing and blessing their own child, about to join her companions. Grandparents and parents lift up their hands and eyes to Heaven on behalf of their darling, whose face bears a look of such humility, and love, and steadfastness, that one turns away from the picture with the sense that one has been standing on hallowed ground.

But the boat which is to take us westward is waiting for us at Lachine, and if we are to arrive at Hamilton next month we must hurry westwards. So, good-bye, Sir Donald, and good-bye to your guests; but *au revoir!*

"The First Communion."

IV.

A CANADIAN LAKE VOYAGE.

THAT was a mistake when I said the boat was waiting for us at Lachine! I must have been thinking of the Lachine Rapids, which are one of the sights which all right-minded visitors to Montreal go and see, and down which they generally descend in a steamer. We had fully intended to include them in our programme, but want of time and heavy rain prevented our going, and so I cannot give you the description of an eye-witness. There are a number of these rapids on the St. Lawrence, those of Lachine being the best known. They presented formidable obstacles to the early explorers, until the Indians guided them over the dangers in their bark canoes. It is said that the safest course for the steamboats to take was discovered by first shooting the rapids on rafts, on the bottom of which were nailed many spikes of wood, and the deepest course was then known by examining which spikes had been broken off by contact with the rocks, and which remained intact.

A somewhat risky experience? But think of the

anxiety which the first captain must have suffered who took a steamer full of passengers down this succession of waterfalls, with rocks which can be touched on either side with a boat-hook. It is not thought much of a feat now, however, when it is done every day in the utmost safety.

We determined to make the most of our last day at Montreal, and so, instead of joining the boat either at Montreal itself or at Lachine, we left late in the afternoon by train to Coteau, about 30 miles west of the city. There we had ordered a "machine" to meet us to drive us for the mile and a half between the station and the river. But our "machine" did not turn up, and we fell to the mercy of a youthful Jehu, with an extremely shaky and antediluvian trap, who took a mischievous pleasure in landing us ever and anon in deep black ruts with which the road abounded, looking back with a twinkle to enjoy the anxious glances of his passengers at the angle in which the frail wheels found themselves during these plunges. But the rough transit did not blind our eyes to the peaceful French Canadian scenes through which we were passing, nor to the gorgeousness of the golden sunset which was glorifying the whole landscape. Soon we were established in our new abode, the "Corsican," with its clean cabins and attentive stewards, and its genial, sailor-like captain, who had been navigating the river for twenty-eight years, but who came originally from Maidenhead. He was good enough to invite us to his own upper deck, near the steersman's cabin, and once having clambered up the precipitous ladder which led thither, we enjoyed a magnificent view. That first evening was lovely; the glow of the sunset melting into full moonlight in an incredibly short space of time, and we sat and sketched, and congratulated ourselves on having taken the boat instead of the hot stuffy train. Next day was too hazy and grey for a proper view of the far famed "Thousand Islands," through which the "Corsican" threaded her passage. No name could better describe the scene than the "Thousand Islands." The broad river, which, at places, is seven miles across, is literally studded with islands of all shapes and sizes, some scarcely more than a rock on which a bush has taken root, others large enough to maintain a small colony. Nearly every island has its villa and its flag, and its little pier with brightly coloured pleasure-boats lying around. Steam launches ply busily from one point to another, whistling importantly their approach, while fishermen are seen pursuing their craft devotedly in every little bay. The air resounds with the laughter of picnic parties; for this is one of the great holiday haunts of the Americans, and at night the villas and the hotels vie one with another as to who can best illuminate their respective islands. It is therefore a gay and attractive scene that the river here presents, but we agreed that it has not the same imposing beauty that we saw further east. But now, in the afternoon, we are approaching Kingston, full of historical associations, from the old days of Frontenac onwards, and which commands the river in a most picturesque way. Our captain told us we could have just two hours ashore, and so we hurried off, desirous first of all to assure ourselves of the well-being of a daughter of one of Lord Aberdeen's tenants who had emigrated hither two or three years back. We found her happy and bright, and quite a Canadian, giving her verdict in favour of the "new

Kingston, Ontario

country" most emphatically. She had been with the same mistress ever since she came out, and appeared to be a great favourite with the latter. Having received this further testimony in favour of the emigration to Canada of the right sort of hard-working girls, we proceeded round the sights of the town, under the guidance of a genuine Irish cabman, who did the honours, impartially of the Barracks, of the Military College, of the Martello Towers, and of the Penitentiary and the Lunatic Asylum and the Queen's College—this latter being a Presbyterian University, presided over by the well-known and eloquent Principal Grant. Then, after a comfy little tea at the hotel, we scurried back in good time before the bell of departure sounded, and we sailed out into Lake Ontario in the rays of the setting sun in the happy delusion that we were to glide over waters as smooth as the river which we had just left, till we found ourselves at Toronto, which we were to reach next morning.

Alas for our hopes! We descended to supper, but scarcely were we seated, than swish-swash came a wave through the port hole, sweeping over glasses and plates in its passage. We do not know much of what happened in the supper saloon after that. We were each alone in our narrow berth bewailing our folly for having trusted the treacherous waters instead of having resorted, bag and baggage, to the train at Kingston. But, at three in the morning, hark, what is that whistle? What is that welcome clanking of a chain? Are we stopping? Yes, indeed. And is there any chance of escape? The thought occurred simultaneously to two passengers, who appeared with wan faces and dishevelled hair at the door of their cabins at the same time, and confronted one another with the same question. The thought was quickly put into action, after Lord Aberdeen had obtained the kindly co-operation of the captain, who even refrained from scoffing at such deserters, and admitted that it had come up a pretty stiff and unexpected gale. And a few minutes later we were left rejoicing on a deserted pier with naught but a tea-kettle, a plaid, and an umbrella in our hands. But a Robinson Crusoe inhabited that pier —as fate would have it, he was Cruso by name—and he was like his namesake in hospitality also, and in his ability for making the best of whatever strangers came his way. He asked not our name or our business, but made us free of the office which he occupied as agent for the steam-boats. He asked us if we wanted anything, he provided us with money, he volunteered to stir up a cab in the town to fetch us to the station a couple of hours later, and he showed us his method of getting water out of the lake by means of a soda-water bottle with a long string round the neck. What say you to this as a specimen of Canadian hospitality and courtesy? The recipients of it were, any way, genuinely grateful, and very joyfully did we balance ourselves on the edge of the pier in the dark, and, in the midst of the gale, fish for water, and then make our tea in the shelter of the office, listening to the storm outside. You will think us very cowardly sailors, I fear; but it is no joke, I assure you; and if you love not a storm at sea, remember our advice and keep to the train when you come out to Canada. Mr Cruso was as good as his word, and in due course a cabman, who had been unwillingly aroused out of his early morning slumbers, appeared, and about

5 A.M. we boarded a train bound West, in which with difficulty we found a corner among the half-awake passengers who had been travelling all night. From the window we caught a glimpse of our poor ship ploughing her way through the waves, and we congratulated ourselves afresh on our escape. We got long before her to Toronto, but not even here at the "Queen City" did we halt. We were to make acquaintance with her a few days later under more auspicious circumstances, and so we only stopped long enough to change from one train to another, which, skirting along a lake, brought us, after an hour's journey, within sight of a most attractive first view of our new Canadian home. You shall not see this view yet. I will but put you down on the platform at Hamilton, and we will go on to "Highfield," and prepare breakfast and a warm welcome for you there.

V

HAMILTON.

I AM sure that any of you who have travelled will agree that one of its chief pleasures is coming home again. And we felt almost like getting home when we walked into the cool, comfortable dining-room, where breakfast had been prepared for us by those of our household who had preceded us to "Highfield," the house which was to be our home whilst in Canada. Here is a picture of Highfield. I will but give you one of Hamilton, for it is a place which photographs do not do full justice to. The town lies on a gently-rising slope round the head of a beautiful bay, and nestles under a steep ridge, which stretches miles and miles away to the heights of Niagara. Here it shelteringly protects the town, which fondly acknowledges its sway, and which demands from all strangers and new-comers a due tribute of loyal admiration for the "Mountain." As an illustration of this admiration, the day after we arrived, a boy, of about thirteen, came up to Lord Aberdeen as he was walking in the grounds, and said, "Is Lord Haddo at home?" "Well, no, he is not, but I am his father, What do you want with him?"

"Well, I wanted to interview him, and ask what his lordship thought of our city, and I wanted to put the interview in my father's newspaper."

Lord Aberdeen was rather startled, in spite of having become somewhat familiarised to the custom of "interviewing" which prevails universally on the other side of the water, by means of which public men make known their views. He had scarcely, however, expected his elevenyear old son to be called upon to give his opinions as yet, and he tried to explain to the youthful journalist that in the old country boys were not expected to air their views so soon. But our young friend was not easily baffled. He still persisted in asking "if Lord Haddo had made arrangements to inspect the public buildings of the city, and especially if he had visited 'the *Mountain*,' and what he thought of *that*." Lord Aberdeen informed him that his boy was at that moment enjoying a clamber up the steep, and did his best to satisfy his enterprising enquirer by expressing his own appreciation of the heights under whose shade they were standing.

Well, climb up this Mountain (almost on the side of which stands Highfield), in the cool of an early September evening, and see the town spreading itself out east and west below you—wide and well-kept streets, trim lawns

Highfield, Hamilton, Ontario

as green as those in England, houses nestling amongst trees, handsome buildings, church spires and factory chimneys competing for pre-eminence. And beyond the city, and its manufactories, and its wharves, lies the bay, all gleaming with the bright colours of the setting sun, amid which little yachts and pleasure boats are making their way home. Our thoughts linger fondly over the restful days spent in this peaceful retreat, and I fancy that both we and our children associate Highfield to a great extent with sunshine and butterflies. Perhaps we had a little more of the former than we cared for just at first—for days with the thermometer over 90 deg. in the shade do not as a rule commend themselves to Scottish-bred folk. But after all we had not much to grumble at, for the heat was not accompanied by our much-dreaded foes, the blood-thirsty mosquitoes. True, this race of pests, who are supposed to avoid Hamilton as a rule, had sent out this year an advance-guard to survey the place, and even we, though late in the season, heard ominous trumpetings as we laid our heads on our pillows, but it seems that as yet they were but vegetarian specimens of the race who had arrived, for none of our party suffered at their hands. Nor did they suffer at ours. We did not capture a single specimen. And this is a great deal to say for such an insect-hunting family as we must confess ourselves to be.

As we sat in the pretty secluded little grounds which

The Gore, Hamilton, Ontario.

surround Highfield that first day, we became conscious that we were by no means alone, and our children, who had joined us, were soon in full pursuit of the wonderful creatures, which looked like butterflies on the wing, but turned into grasshoppers when they alighted, of the "Camberwell Beauties," and the "Admirals," and the many other brightly-coloured visitors of our garden. But we did not do much that first day—we had not the necessary implements, and we had to sally forth in search of the wherewithall to make butterfly nets, and killing-boxes, and specimen boxes, and I know not what. (And here, by way of a parenthesis, I must beg the readers of "WEE WILLIE WINKIE," who look in here, to understand that we are a family of scientific entomologists, that we employ the most humane methods in killing our victims, that we should look with horror on any one who should stick pins through them alive, and that we do not kill those we do not need for our cabinet. Pray forgive this parenthesis, good readers. I feared that we might be confounded with the cruel boy whom our magazine has held up to reprobation.)

And here let me introduce the four young butterfly-hunters of Highfield. Of course if you ever hear that their mother—your staid editor—joined them in their wild pursuit of her majesty the glorious red-winged swift-flying "Queen of Spain," or if you hear of her anointing telegraph poles and trees with honey and

Lord Haddo. Aged 11.

Lady Marjorie H. Gordon. Aged 9.

molasses, and flitting about with others of the staff of "ONWARD AND UPWARD" at dead of night, with lanterns, capturing unwary, but magnificent moths, who had imbibed the sweet draughts too freely, you will surely not believe such tales!

Suffice it to say that a really beautiful collection of moths and butterflies resulted from our stay at Highfield,

Hon. Dudley and Hon. Archie H. Gordon.   Aged 6 and 5.

a collection doomed to an untimely end, for during their transitho me, they got so battered, that it was only left to mother and daughter to mingle their tears together over their ashes. We must not ask you to linger with us in our lamentations over our broken treasures. We live in hope of replacing them some day, and meanwhile we have other memories of Hamilton which we wish to share with you.

A Hamilton Yacht.

A hundred years ago Hamilton had barely begun to exist. But the few who were then ploughing up the land on which the city now stands were of the stamp which makes nations to rejoice over her children. You will remember that after the war which resulted in the independence of the United States, a number of American people, who had remained true to the British flag throughout the war, resolved to give up their lands and their homes and migrate to Canada, rather than dwell in a land which had revolted from the Crown to which they were so loyal. And England right joyfully held out her arms to these noble-hearted refugees. Ontario was then unpeopled, and so two hundred acres of land in this rich province were granted free to every one of these United Empire Loyalists, as they were called. U.E. Loyalists they are now usually designated, and those who can trace their parentage to these families count it a proud descent, and glory in it.

> " And they who have loved
> The cause that had been lost, and kept their faith
> To England's Crown, and scorned an alien name,
> Passed into exile; leaving all behind
> Except their honour, and the conscious pride
> Of duty done to country and to King.
> Broad lands, ancestral homes, the gathered wealth
> Of patient toil and self-denying years
> Were confiscate and lost; for they had been
> The salt and savour of the land, trained up
> In honour, loyalty, and fear of God.
> . . . .

"Not drooping like poor fugitives, they came
In exodus to our Canadian wilds:
But full of heart and hope, with heads erect
And fearless eyes, victorious in defeat.
With thousand toils they forced their devious way
Through the great wilderness of silent woods
That gloomed o'er lake and stream; till higher rose
The northern star above the broad domain
Of half a continent, still theirs to hold,
Defend, and keep forever as their own;
Their own and England's, to the end of time.

. . . .

"King's gifts upon the exiles were bestowed.
Ten thousand homes were planted; and each one,
With axe and fire, and mutual help, made war
Against the wilderness, and smote it down.
Into the open glades, unlit before,
Since forests grew, or rivers ran, there leaped
The sun's bright rays, creating heat and light,
Waking to life the buried seeds that slept
Since time's beginning, in the earth's dark womb.

. . . .

"To keep the empire one in unity
And brotherhood of its imperial race,
For that they nobly fought and bravely lost,
Where losing was to win a higher fame!
In building up our northern land to be
A vast Dominion stretched from sea to sea—
A land of labour, but of sure reward—
A land of corn to feed the world withal—
A land of life's rich treasures, plenty, peace;
Content and freedom, both to speak and do,
A land of men to rule with sober law
This part of Britain's Empire, next to the heart,
Loyal as were their fathers and as free!"

—Kirby.

One of the earliest of these refugees was Robert Laud, and he selected the head of the lake, more because of the game to be found there, and the scenery, than because of the fertility of the soil. His first acre was ploughed with a hoe, sown with a bushel of wheat, and harrowed with a leafy bough. He was his own miller, too, for some years, until a French-Canadian arrived and set up a mill some seven miles away. Then other farmers came, and in 1813 George Hamilton laid out his farm in village lots, and gave the future town its name. Lying as it does so near the frontier, it did not escape anxious times during the war of 1812 and the following years, and in 1832 it narrowly escaped destruction at the hands of a terrible visitation of the cholera, and the same year by a raging fire. These trials did but prove the mettle of the inhabitants of the young town, and perhaps furnish the reason why its streets are now so broad, and so cared for, its buildings so solid, its sanitary arrangements so thoroughly looked into, its provisions against destruction by fire so complete. A popular writer described Hamilton in 1858 as "the ambitious and stirring little city," and the name stuck; only "little" she is no longer, being the third city in the Dominion, having a population of over 50,000, and her critics have missed out the "stirring," so if you seek for news of Hamilton in the general newspapers, you must look for it under the heading "The Ambitious City." But she is not, and

View on Hamilton Bay.

need not, be ashamed of this nickname, for she has shown herself ambitious to some purpose. I could take up a large part of these Canadian talks by describing to you the public buildings and their uses, the magnificent school buildings and the good work that goes on in them, the institutions—social, literary, philanthropic, and religious—the many manufactories, which cause this town to be regarded as the Birmingham of Canada, the acres of vineyards around the fruit gardens and orchards, which give this part of the country the name of "the Garden of Canada," the churches of all denominations whose services we attended, and above all the people, of Hamilton. But, having regard to the length and purport of these sketches, I will not launch into so large a subject. Suffice it to say that the kindness and good fellowship extended to us by the inhabitants of Hamilton, of all classes, did what only true hearty courtesy and kindness can do, viz., we felt ourselves to be no mere tourists and strangers, but fellow-citizens of "no mean city." And in proof of this assertion, I have, by my side here, in the office of "ONWARD AND UPWARD," two beautifully-bound books, concerning the birds and plants of Canada, and which were presented to me by the Free Library Committee, as being the first citizen to apply for a book, on the occasion of Lord Aberdeen's opening of the new buildings. (I must confide to you, however, that your President's character had to be inquired into before I was admitted as a reader. I had to produce a certificate of character for honesty, and so forth, signed by two citizens of Hamilton. You will be glad to know that I found two Senators willing to vouch for me !)

There is no doubt that if you want really to know something of a country, its customs, and its people, it is a great advantage if you can settle down in some typical place for a few weeks, instead of merely travelling through and seeing the sights of each town. In the latter way you may see more perhaps of the buildings, institutions, &c., for if you have but a day or two, you map out your time, and spend it in driving from one place to another, and you thus get through a great deal: but if you make yourself at home anywhere for a bit, you will not do the tourist so much, but if you mix at all with the people, you almost unconsciously get to understand them and their ways of thinking, and the why and wherefore of their customs and institutions. This was our experience, living our every-day life, interchanging visits, reading the daily papers of all sections of politics, mingling with clergy, statesmen, merchants, agriculturists, &c., and hearing various opinions from all sorts and conditions of men. And the sum total of what we learnt made us feel that the more the old country learnt to know her grown-up child over the sea, the more she would be proud of her in all ways, and the more earnestly did it make us wish and pray that the future of Canada may be worthy of her past, and that the present God-fearing, industrious, simple, education-loving stock may only be reinforced by those worthy to combine with them in building up a grand nation and country.

As I have said before, none need fear to go out to Canada who are ready to work. Our lads and lasses who went out with us with the intention of settling (and of whom I give you a group sitting outside " Highfield "), have nearly all found happy homes. One, indeed, has come back because of her father's death, but I feel much tempted to give you extracts from some of the letters of others. They have not suffered at all from the cold of the winter, but seem to have enjoyed the merry winter customs, and seeing all the skating and the sleighing going on round about them. For one thing, the heartiness of Canadians towards new-comers counts for a great deal: they do all they can to make everyone feel welcome and one with them—there is a freeness, a sense of equality, a consciousness that everyone will be taken just for what he or she is worth, and nothing more or less, which cannot altogether be attained in the old world, and which must always be refreshing to anyone of independent spirit. " Prove yourself to be a man, a woman, and we shall respect you, and you shall have an equal chance with any of us, and what is more, we will do our best to put you into the running with us from the first."

The Lads and Lasses who accompanied us to Highfield, and remained in Canada.

Human nature is undoubtedly the same everywhere, and Canadians would not wish to claim for themselves immunity from all faults, but they may fairly claim that anyone wishing to live a free, independent, self-respecting, law-abiding, and God-fearing life, has as few impediments under the government, the public life and customs, the bright climate, and the sanguine temperament of Canada and her folk as they will find in any land under the sun.

Lord Aberdeen was accused of distributing, in some of his speeches in Canada, what was termed "taffy to the Dominion." (Is this word derived from "toffee," I wonder? Anyway it means something sweet.) Perhaps I shall be accused of following in his footsteps. Well, we can only speak of that we do know, and what we have seen, and I can honestly say that I am not conscious of having flattered. Next month I invite you to accompany us to some of Canada's autumn fairs, and to see some of her products.

VI.

TORONTO.

WHAT a rash promise I made last month! I believe I promised to escort you to some of the well-known Autumn Fairs of Canada, and now that the time has come for me to fulfil my promise, and I have begun to look up my notes, my heart misgives me, and I have almost a mind to throw you over. For how can I do justice to all that we saw? It is one thing to be guided and another thing to guide. But it is of no use making excuses. I must just do my best; so come along, to begin with, to the greatest of Canadian Fairs, in the "Queen City" of Toronto. And we had begun to feel ourselves quite familiar with Toronto, for in our house at Hamilton was a telephone, not only communicating with nearly every other house in the town, and thus saving many a note and interview, but having also communication with Toronto on the one side, 40 miles east of us, and London on the other, about 30 miles west. (Yes, London; I mean what I say—London on the Thames, in the county of Middlesex. Look in your geography books and you will find there is more than one London in the world, and when you go to Canada you will learn always to explain *which* London you mean—London, England, or London, Ontario. But, indeed, we have found ourselves that the more youthful of the two Londons has already made its existence known in the Old World, for when we were in Italy last year, and wanted on one occasion to send a telegram to London, we simply addressed it to London, without adding England. But a message came back to ask whether it was London in England or in Canada that we meant!)

But our first real personal acquaintance with Toronto was made on the opening day of what is familiarly known in the country as "Canada's Greatest Fair." Here every autumn congregate thousands and thousands of agriculturists, fruit-raisers, manufacturers, and pleasure-seekers. The Fair goes on for a fortnight, and is held in grounds of 60 acres of public land, specially set apart for the purpose for two months in the year, and on which handsome buildings have been erected for exhibition purposes, and are maintained by the Exhibition Committee. These grounds are found too small now for the exhibition of all the stock that is brought from all parts of the Dominion, not to speak of the agricultural machinery in which Canada excels, and the specimens of manufactured goods of every description, from pianos and organs, and really beautiful articles of furniture, down to the humblest of household necessaries. And not only the useful was

University Buildings, Toronto.

provided for, but the ornamental, and the amusing also, were given their full place. Trotting races, the Wild West Show—a performance after the manner of Buffalo Bill, with cow-boys and wild Indians and buck-jumping horses, and side performances of all kinds—were all to hand for the diversion of those who were not interested in the all-absorbing agricultural work and prospects of the country. And in spite of the vast concourse of people assembling daily (it is reckoned that 300,000 visitors attended the Fair each week), there was a remarkable absence of any disorderly conduct or unseemly language. All strangers are struck by the good behaviour of the crowd, and by the evidence it gives of the high moral tone prevailing in Canada, and which, amongst other results, shews itself in a popular agreement that no intoxicating drinks shall be sold on the grounds during the Fair. Lord Aberdeen had the honour done him to be asked to open this vast Exhibition, and to give an address on the occasion, and it was then that we first visited Toronto, and that we were first brought into contact with a Canadian crowd. The opening ceremony is somewhat a trying one, for it takes place in the open air, the speakers occupying a platform given up afterwards to acrobats and jugglers, and having to address a vast crowd in an amphitheatre opposite, with the racing-course intervening. The ordeal, however, was safely got through, and the audience were very kind, and appeared satisfied.

But I must return to our Toronto Fair, and I feel I ought to take you round the Dog Show, and the Poultry Show, and the Honey Show, all of which were excellent; and then I ought to tell you of all the strange implements for sowing, and reaping, and binding, and digging, and I do not know what besides; and then we ought to see the roots and the vegetables, and the magnificent show of fruit; and then we ought to stand in the ring, and see the Herefords, and the Shorthorns, and our own Aberdeen-Angus cattle being led out, and seeming very much at home, and the Clydesdales, too, and the roadsters, and the wonderful jumping-horse "Rosebery," who cleared the seven-feet jump easily. Besides there are the Manitoba exhibits, and those from the North-West and British Columbia. And there are the birds, and the insects, and the snakes to be seen. Well, what do you say to going through all these shows, and my pointing out the merits of each exhibit? If you were wise you would not absolutely trust yourself to my knowledge on all these subjects, even though I had the benefit of being shown all by our most kind friend, Captain Macmaster, Vice-President of the Fair. But even if you would, I am afraid you would not care for a *whole* number of the Magazine to be devoted to Canada, which would be the result of your rashness, and if you or any of your friends want to know more in detail about the agricultural resources of the country, I would advise you to write to the High Commissioner for Canada, 17 Victoria Street, London, S.W., and ask for some of the reports on Canada made by the British tenant-farmers, who went out in 1891, on the invitation of the Canadian Govern-

Captain Macmaster.

ment and visited every part of the country, and who have made most valuable reports on all they had seen, for the use of those wanting full and reliable information.

Some of these tenant-farmers were present at the Toronto Fair the same day as we were (on our second visit), and we saw them going about everywhere making notes.

But I have told you nothing yet of our host at Govern-

Government House, Toronto.

ment House, where we stayed for the night. We had had the good fortune to be fellow-passengers across the Atlantic with the Lieutenant-Governor of Ontario, Sir Alexander Campbell,* and he had proved the best and

* Sir Alexander Campbell died in May 1892, after these letters were published.

kindest of friends, both as regards bodily and mental wants, for as to the former, he had made us free of his private provision of tea and butter, and Devonshire cream, and as to the latter, he told us much which enabled us to feel that we knew a good deal about

*Sir Alexander Campbell,
late Lieutenant-Governor of Ontario.*

Canada before we got there. He has lived a long life of public usefulness to his adopted country, and we count the friendship with which he honoured us as one of the solid gains which our trip to Canada brought us. And now, he and his daughter, Miss Marjorie Campbell, took care of us in their pleasant Government House, and through their kindness we made other friends—amongst others, Mr Mowat, the Hon. Prime Minister of Ontario, and the Speaker of the Dominion Senate, the Hon. Mr Allan; and we renewed acquaintance with our friend, Mr Edward Blake, one of the leaders of the Opposition, and a well-known orator and statesman. Then Sir Alexander drove me all round the city next morning, and showed me the new and the old parts, the Queen's Park, and the different colleges and schools, and the beautiful University Buildings, which were in large parts destroyed by fire last year. They still presented a grand appearance, and I am happy to say they are to be worthily restored.

Now for a peep at the London Fair, and then both you and I must have a rest. A bad cold unfortunately prevented me from accompanying Lord Aberdeen to London, as I much wanted to do, but he came home full of praise of the bright appearance of this young city of 35,000 inhabitants, which goes by the name of the "Forest City," on account of the great number of trees planted along the well-laid broad streets. I have given you two peeps of London and its surroundings, but must leave you to imagine the rest, as I cannot give a personal report. But one thing I can tell you. Just after we left Canada, a very spirited little monthly paper for women was started in London, called *Wives and Daughters*. If ever any of you go to Canada I advise you to take it in, and meanwhile I hope to give you extracts from it now and again. And now, Good-night, ladies and gentlemen. I hope that my inefficiency as a guide to the agricultural fairs will not prevent you from allowing me to conduct you to the Falls of Niagara, and then to Canada's capital, and then we must hie away West. But now once more, Good-night!

VII.

OTTAWA.

ON second thoughts, I think we had better not linger at Niagara. You must have heard it described so often, and have seen so many pictures of it, that we should be going over what you would *feel* to be well-known ground. So I will only give you a little picture of these wonderful falls, and then pass on. Only do not you ever think that you can have the slightest conception of what "the Falls" are really like until you have been there, until you have stood and gazed at them, and have looked at them from this point and from that, above and below, here where they are about to precipitate themselves in a wild surging flood over the cliffs, and there where the mighty volume of water, having poured itself down over the crags and rocks in grand magnificence, convulses itself into terrific and seemingly useless fury in its efforts to make its way along its course. Watch, and look, and listen to the roar of many waters, and go back again and again, and then you will know what you have felt Niagara to mean, though you may never be able to describe it.

It is the Niagara district that shares with that immediately round Hamilton, the distinction of producing the finest fruit in the Dominion, as well as the greatest quantity. And we found that reputation to be in no wise exaggerated when we visited the Fair at Hamilton and saw the rows and rows of apples and pears, and peaches, of all sizes and descriptions; and then the grapes! Why have I not a photograph to show you the long piled-up tables, covered with lovely clusters of bloom-covered grapes! The "Niagara" white grape is supposed to be the best of the varieties of Canadian open-air grapes, all of which have a taste somewhat peculiar to themselves and not liked by everybody. Speaking from experience, I can only say that we thought we had never tasted better grapes in our lives, than some which we gathered, growing in a perfectly wild state up the cliffs, near Dundas, where we had scrambled up in pursuit of butterflies and a most splendid view. Some day you will have a better chance of tasting Canadian-grown grapes when more special arrangements are made for their conveyance by the steamers. As it is, if you want the best apples in the market, you will always ask for "Niagara" apples. But we are lingering too long in the fruit orchards of Ontario, and we must repair to the station again at Hamilton and take our tickets for Ottawa, the capital of the Dominion; for Ottawa, which, some twenty-five years ago, went by the name of Bye-

Falls of Niagara

town, a Hudson Bay Company station and a centre for the lumberers. Now at a distance we see the proud towers of the Parliament Houses and Government Buildings, commanding the heights above the river, and we see a town which, though far smaller than Montreal,

Above Niagara.

or Toronto, or even Hamilton, can well challenge comparison in point of her picturesque situation, and one which must, from all accounts, be a centre of brightness and mirth all through the merry Canadian winter She owes her position as capital to the fact that when all the

View of Ottawa

different provinces in Canada were confederated into one Dominion in 1866, there was too much jealousy between the great cities of Montreal and Toronto to allow of either of these being chosen, and so the Queen

Lord Stanley.

chose the little Indian town of Ottawa, standing on the confines of Quebec and Ontario, to be the centre of Government. We spent some most interesting days

Ottawa. 77

here. I will but mention our visit to Sir John Macdonald, and the kindness with which he received us, for I cannot attempt a task which would take too long, viz., to tell you about the statesmen and leaders of political life in Canada

Lady Stanley.

at whose hands we received kindness. They were good enough to gather at a dinner given to Lord Aberdeen later on, and both then and at all times they did all in their power to make our visit combine both instruction and pleasure. You will have noticed in the papers that after Sir John Macdonald's death, before Sir John Abbott became Premier, Sir John Thompson, the Minister of Justice, was first summoned by the Governor-General to form a Government. We had the chance of making Sir John and Lady Thompson's acquaintance in the steamer which took us across the Atlantic, and we and our Kodak did our best to take photographs of them, but I am sorry to say that that best on that occasion was a failure, and so you are cheated of pictures which we should have much liked to reproduce in our Magazine, and which would have reminded us of many pleasant talks.

At Ottawa, as elsewhere in the Dominion, the Scotch element is strong; and at the house of our kind friend Sir James Grant (or, as we should delight to call him in Inverness-shire, "Corrymony," which is the old home of his family, and the laird of which he is by descent) and Lady Grant, where we were introduced to a number of prominent citizens, we found that not a few claimed Scottish birth or parentage. Under Sir James's escort, too, we visited the beautifully-arranged Geological Museum, where we were shown specimens of all the valuable minerals that lie buried in Canadian soil, and which will enrich many future generations. We saw, too, samples of the beautiful precious stones which

Canada can produce for her children, Labradorites, and Sodorites, and Perthites, and Asterias, all radiating with beautiful soft blues and purples, and golden and silver colours. They have not yet become fashionable, but

Sir John Abbott, Prime Minister of Canada, 1891-92.

when they are known their time will come. Then we went upstairs and saw the cases of birds and butterflies, and Lord Aberdeen brought away with him two lovely little stuffed owls, not more than five inches high, and these little owls now look down on me from the top of

A pair of Aceedian or San-whet Owls.

my bookcase at home, and exhort me to be as wise as they are. But we brought something else besides these wee owls back from Ottawa. Of course a "Fair" was going on here too, and after the parade of cattle and of cart horses came some pairs of fast trotting carriage horses, and among these were a pair of black horses which Lord Aberdeen admired so much that he bought

Canadian Dick and Bill at Dollis Hill, Willesden.

them, and sent them home. These are our friends, Dick and Bill, about whom our little girl wrote in the Children's Page of the January number of ONWARD AND UPWARD. They are dear, kind horses, and understand what is said to them very well. They go very fast, and take us up to London from our little farm at Dollis Hill, fully five miles away, in half-an-hour easily. Here they are, ready to start.

At the Ottawa Fair we also had the opportunity of making acquaintance with the Hon. Mr Carling, Minister for Agriculture. He was good enough to offer to take us to see the Government Experimental Farm he had established about three miles from the town. So on a glorious September afternoon we drove out, in company with Mr Carling and Mr Mackintosh, one of the Members of Parliament for the city, another kind friend of ours. The Farm was taken in hand by Mr Carling about four years ago, and scarcely a day passes when he is at Ottawa without his visiting it. There are about 500 acres in all; but it is not yet all cultivated. Experiments of all sorts are carried on here relative to seeds, feeding-stuffs, flowers, fruit, vegetables, trees, poultry, cattle, sheep, pigs, horses, &c., &c., and the results of the experiments are published from time to time. The farmers from all over the Dominion can send their seeds here to be tested as to fertility, nutritiousness, &c.; and this they can do free of cost, for the Post-Office carries everything addressed to and from the Experimental Farm free. And the farmers are largely taking advantage of the opportunities thus afforded them, and are cultivating their farms according to the advice given, and so far the results have been found satisfactory. Then, again, seeds are sent to careful farmers in the various provinces for them to test in their various localities and climate, and to report upon. We saw at the Farm various houses and plots of ground where experiments were being carried on, and we saw also a dairy in process of construction, where they are to test the produce of various breeds of cows as to milking powers, and the different methods of making butter, cheese, &c. Experiments are also being made as to the expense of feeding animals. To illustrate this Mr Saunders, the energetic manager, showed us some splendid, sleek, healthy-looking Clydesdales, which were fed at a cost of only 15 cents a day (about 8d.), by having their hay and all their food chopped up, and not wasted in any way. I will not, however, keep those of you who are not interested in agricultural matters longer at what we found to be a most engrossing place; nor will I tell you just now of the half-hour spent with Mr Fletcher, who superintends the entomological and gardening departments, and who makes researches as to the insects which are injurious and those that are beneficial, and how to keep down the former and encourage the latter.

No, we must hurry off to see some of the saw-mills at work, which are one of the sights of Ottawa. As you look on the enchanting view down the river, from the high terrace outside the Parliament Houses, you see thousands and thousands of huge piles of sawn planks, and when you go down amongst them, you walk through them as through narrow streets of high buildings, and you wonder how there can ever be enough demand for

The View from the Terrace outside Parliament Buildings, Ottawa.

all this wood. Both by day and night (by the use of the electric light) do the huge saw-mills work on, replenishing and increasing these vast stores of wood, which are destined to travel to all parts of the world. It is a wonderful thing to stand in one of these mills, vibrating with the workings of the mighty engines working the huge saws and blades, and full of busy workers moving between the machinery, which is acting out its relentless will on each victim from the far away woods which it receives into its jaws. You see these huge forest trees, cut down hundreds of miles away, each marked with its owner's brand, floated down the river, and guided down the rushing water to the special mill to which it belongs. In a moment it is hauled up, dripping, and dark, and rough, and it is under the steel teeth of the huge monster—a crash and a hiss, and in a few moments, after having run the gauntlet of one machine after another, the king of the forest emerges out of the other end of the shed, a pile of common-place looking planks. "Lumbering," as it is called, has been one of the chief industries of Canada during the last fifty years, and young men loving a rough adventurous life have delighted in its freedom, its variety, and its dangers. The lumberers live amongst the forests in rough shanties all through the winter, felling the trees, and marking them, and taking them down all sorts of precipitous slides, called "skidways," through snow, and ice, and drifts, to the water's edge. Their dress is rough, they sleep in a blanket on a bunk, and their food consists for the most part of pork and home-made bread, and huge potions of tea (no intoxicating drinks are ever allowed at the shanties), but they seem to be none the worse for their hardships. As they work they shout the merry lumberers' songs, and now and again they have a chance of using the rifles which lie always ready to hand, and they get some fresh venison as a reward of their skill. They also trap bears occasionally. The trap is formed of an enclosure of stakes driven into the ground. A log is then suspended above, propped up by a stick to which the bait is attached, and when poor " Mr Bruin" is unwary enough to seize the tempting dainty he is done for!

When spring comes, the lumberman's duties alter. They have to see that the logs brought down to the water's edge get properly into the current, that none get caught by the rocks or other impediments, and the dangers encountered in driving down timber like this are very considerable, although the skill of the men in jumping from log to log in the water, in guiding them with their long hooks, and in running their flat-bottomed boats down the rapids, is very remarkable. On rivers where large cataracts occur, artificial channels are made, called "slides." These are lined with timber, and at the upper end gates are put up through which the pent-up water can be admitted or shut off. Down these "slides" pass the "cribs," which are formed of logs fastened together with large pieces of timber on the top. Often a rough wooden hut is also fixed on the crib for the raftsmen, who guide their craft either with long oars, called "sweepers," or put up a sail on an improvised

Rideau Hall, Ottawa, the residence of the Governor-General.

mast. There is one of these slides near Ottawa, on which visitors are taken who desire to have the sensation of "shooting a slide." When you embark above the crib-gates, you are bidden to take a firm hold of a pole fastened on to the logs beneath; the gates are thrown open; the water surges over; the crib, carefully steered through the gateway, advances over the entrance, and then leaps with a rush down the narrow channel till it reaches the calm water below. We did not ourselves taste the pleasures of the plunge, but have taken this account of it from an article on "Lumbering," by Principal Grant, in *Picturesque Canada*. The sensation must be much the same as that enjoyed by the Canadian tobogganers, whose sport reigns supreme among the many winter amusements. We visited Rideau Hall, the residence of the Governor-General, and saw the high toboggan-slide put up by the Marquis of Lorne, of which we here give you a picture, which is the centre of so much bright, healthy fun. I need not describe to you what a toboggan is, for you see it here in its rapid headlong descent, with its laughing, breathless freight, and the mischances and tumbles, and occasions for merriment to which its voyagers are exposed. Here I shall leave you a while to amuse yourselves, or to wait to see one of the Governor's toboggan parties by torchlight, and if you get tired of this, try your hand at our old Scotch game of curling, for which you will find ample

The Toboggan-Slide at Rideau Hall

facilities hard by, or try your snow-shoes, or summon a sleigh and have a bewitching drive to the sound of the jangling bells along the smooth, dry, hard, snow-covered roads. I go to prepare our car for our Westward trip.

VIII.

ACROSS THE PRAIRIES.

NOW, in with you, if you do not want to be left behind! And please remember that you have to keep your wits about you during this journey when you get out at railway stations. We have left the whistles behind us in the old country, and in their stead you hear a bell, which at first reminds you more than anything else of the bell of a country church or school, and when you hear that bell, scramble in as best you can, for there will be no slamming of carriage doors, no crying of "Take your seats," no guard's whistle as a last warning. The conductor calls "All aboard," but if the train is a long one, you are as likely as not to miss hearing him. And at every station where we stop you will see after the train has actually started, a rush of stragglers scrambling up on the "platforms" at either end of the long cars. Of course you know that trains in America are not at all like those in this country. Here you have a picture of our car, and all the carriages are constructed on this principal with a platform at each end, over which

92   Through Canada with a Kodak.

you can pass when the train is in motion. People walk from one carriage to another, and during the long

"*All Aboard!*"

Across the Prairies. 93

journeys dining-cars are attached at certain hours of the day, where passengers can go and have their meals, and feel very much as if they were in a moving hotel. Little tables for two or four people are placed down each side

The Car in which we travelled West.

of the long car, the waiters move up and down the passage between the tables, and the kitchen is at one end. Cooking under these circumstances must be rather difficult, but in our experience the results were very satisfactory. When we had our first meal on board one of these cars, we thought that we must be specially fortunate in having an out-of-the-way well managed car attached to the train; but, as we went further, and new cars came on every day, we found that the rule was for everything to be well done, for the attendants to be courteous and obliging. This is only one illustration of the fact that if you hear that the Canadian-Pacific Railway has undertaken to do anything, whether it concerns the piercing of the Rocky Mountains or the making of good soup, you may be sure that it will be well and thoroughly done. Now this is saying a good deal, and moreover, we can guarantee that it is true according to our *experience*, and not merely according to the words of advertising agents and attractive little guide-books, which at times are rather deceptive. Certainly we ought to speak up for that railway if anyone ought, for we were royally treated by being provided with a beautiful new car all to ourselves, in which we could shut ourselves off into comfortable little rooms at night, when partitions were put up, and curtains drawn, and beds pulled down by our faithful porter, John (who ministered to all our wants most assiduously), and during the day could be used as one long sitting-room, panelled with pretty white mahogany, where we read, and wrote, and painted, and where we had many a pleasant little tea-party during the four weeks while we inhabited it.

We thought we had chosen quite the best time of year for our trip, although it might be considered a little late

Across the Prairies. 95

by some, for when we woke up the first morning after leaving Ottawa, we found ourselves passing through roads all flaming with the gorgeous autumnal tints of the maple

John Barber, our Car-Porter.

and other trees, and underneath the trailing leaves of various berry-bearing plants made a carpet of rich yellows, and reds, and browns. I think, if I am to be truthful, I must admit that this scenery would have borne rather a forbidding aspect if it had not been for these rich colourings, and we can scarcely wonder if newly-arrived emigrants bound Westward feel rather depressed at passing through a stretch of such apparently sterile country

A Young Settlement.

at the outset of their journey. The trees are stunted, the vegetation allows us to see the stony character of the soil below; some of the telegraph poles even have to be upheld by heaps of stones around them, and the desolation is often rendered greater by many of the trees having been the prey of forest fires, the result either of

Across the Prairies.

the carelessness of settlers or Indians, or arising from sparks from the engine falling on the dry inflammable substances all around. And yet this region has charms of its own—the fishermen can tell of the wealth to be found in the rivers and lakes, the geologist and the miner will tell you of the yet comparatively unexplored riches of silver and copper and other metals which are stored up for Canada's children beneath the unpromising looking surface, and the artist will revel in the wild grandeur of the mountain and lake scenery all along the coast of Lake Superior. A succession of magnificent promontories, frowning rocks and crags, surrounding the lovely bay of that vast expanse of water calling itself a lake, meets your eye as the train bears you along, and you lay down your pencil and brush in bewilderment as to which point to seize amidst so much beauty, and instead, you revert to the faithful rapid Kodak to record your memories of Thunder Bay, and Jackfish Bay, and the Lake of the Woods, and many another spot of beauty. And then one day as you wake up and peep out behind the blind of your car, the mountain, and the lake, and the torrent have disappeared, and instead you behold a vast stretch of grassy country, and you realise that you see before you the far-famed wheat-lands of Manitoba, and that Winnipeg, the City of Prairies, lies hard by.

At Winnipeg we felt almost as if we had a home awaiting us, for our friend, Sir Donald Smith, about whose generosity to his native country I have told you before, had written to us even before we left England, and had bidden us to come to his house at Silver Heights, and to make ourselves at home. And so, on the verandah of Silver Heights we were assembled with my

Mr O'Brien (who christened the Lake of Killarney) and his wife talking to Lord Aberdeen.

brother (who met us here), and Mr Traill, Sir Donald's manager. Here, too, are Sir Donald's buffaloes, the last remaining in Canada of the millions who used to inhabit the prairies, and whose bones you still see in dismal heaps as you pass along.

Across the Prairies. 99

And now, what am I to say about Winnipeg? It is 700 feet above the sea level, it has a population of 28,000 (twenty years ago there were only 215 inhabitants), it has some fine buildings, wide streets, it is lighted

All that is left of the buffalo.

with electric light, it is a great railway centre, and is destined to become a great capital. You still, however, can see how recent is its birth, for side by side with a fine house stands an old Red River settler's log hut, the wide streets are still mostly unpaved, and on a wet day serve as admirable illustrations of the richness and the blackness of Manitoba soil, and you still see passing through the city by the side of a carriage and pair, the old Red River carts made entirely of wood, creaking as they go. The rate of progress amazes the inhabitants themselves, and it is very pleasant to hear stories of things as they were and as they are. For instance, look at this dog-carriage; that is the vehicle in which the Governor and his wife used to be transported to Ottawa not so many years ago. Rather a different business now-a-days, is it not? We must not linger long here, much as I should like to tell you of the many impressions left on our minds by Winnipeg, its inhabitants and its surroundings, and of all the truly Scotch hospitality with which we were entertained whilst there, and again on our return journey, not only by Sir Donald Smith, and the Lieut.-Governor, Mr Schultz, and his wife, but by many other friends of whose kindness we cherish grateful memories.

One of the impressions most strongly left on our minds by our stay in Winnipeg was the strongly marked religious tone of the community. This is not only shown by the number of churches and religious institutions, but in the evident earnestness of purpose, which causes people who have but little spare time in this young city, to devote themselves to active works of religion and benevolence. The great scarcity of servants often throws a

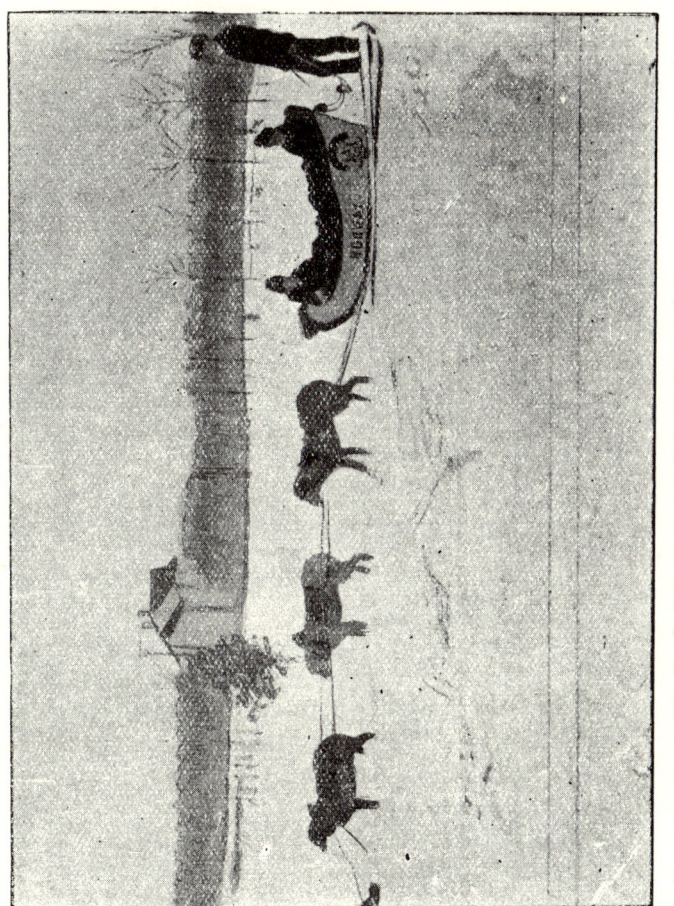

How a journey from Winnipeg for Ottawa was accomplished in days gone by.

large part of the household work on the ladies themselves, and yet they contrive to throw themselves into Christian work, and to take charge personally of the orphans and the aged poor, and to befriend the stranger in a way which may well put us to shame. One of their latest organisations undertakes to send out monthly parcels of literature to settlers in Manitoba and the North-West. It is difficult for those at home to realise the isolation of such settlers; everything has to be begun and carried on by the work of their own hands, and their whole thoughts are absorbed by the desperately hard work which is an essential for success. Church is far away, there are no libraries or reading-rooms or means of self-improvement at hand, and the temptation must be great in such lives to forget mind and soul in the struggle for material prosperity. Those who stay at home and have friends in these distant parts should remember that no greater kindness can be shewn than by sending out good weekly newspapers and magazines, perhaps a picture now and again to brighten up the walls of the wooden house, perhaps some flower seeds from the garden at home, which will bring tender thoughts to the minds of those now so far away, and who will teach their children to tend the little plants sent by "grannie" or "auntie," and so make them think of doing their best to make their homes beautiful and home-like. Frugality, and self-denial, and strength of character are developed by the stern life which must be led by the settler in Manitoba who means to prosper. It is our part to do our best to prevent the possibility of these sterner virtues from becoming too stern, and from growing into a mere passion to get on and to make money. And if you have no friends in Canada yourselves, may I ask those who are willing to do so to save up their papers, and pictures, and magazines, and to send them to—*Madame Gautier, the L.A. Association for distributing Literature to Settlers, Winnipeg, Manitoba.* The ladies of this Association are deluged with applications for monthly packets of such literature, and find that packets containing consecutive issues of the same magazine are those most valued. They will be very gratified for all contributions, helpful for mind, and heart and soul, and tending to give thoughts which will uplift the common daily work which would otherwise be drudgery.

Now let me tell you of a visit we paid to some new settlers from Scotland who are amongst those who need help and sympathy to be shown in this way. And first I will quote from a letter from Sir George Baden Powell to the *Daily Graphic* to explain how they came over from Scotland :—

THE EMIGRATION FUND.

The general public—and so many are now-a-days interested in emigration and colonisation—will remember that the scheme was inaugurated in 1888, when the Government finally decided to offer

£10,000 if another £2000 was given by private charity. At first the Fund was administered by the Scotch Office, under the personal guidance of Lord Lothian, but in the second year a special Colonisation Board was appointed, consisting of representatives of the Imperial and Canadian Governments, the private subscribers, and the land companies aiding the experiment. The proposal was

Manitou, Manitoba.

to select and import to Manitoba such families among the crofters as might apply. It was estimated that a sum of £120 per family would be sufficient to establish them on the 160-acre lots offered them by Canada. This sum was to be eventually repaid by each family, security being meanwhile given by a mortgage on the holding and on the goods and chattels.

THE FIRST SENT OUT.

In May, 1888, eighteen families were despatched, and twelve more families followed in June of the same year. In April, 1889, forty-nine families were sent out. The journey from Scotland to Manitoba was accomplished not without grumbling on the part of the discontented. The first parties were sent rather late in the season, and extra efforts had to be made to provide them with necessaries for the first winter. Many of the crofters gave evidence at once of an indolent reliance on charity, and maintained that Government was to find a home for, and even clothe them. But the spirit of the country soon fell upon them; there was work and hope in the atmosphere; by the second year actual crops gave earnest for the future, and by the third, with its excellent harvest, indolence and grumbling had been completely pushed aside and forgotten, in habits of hard work and confidence in a future of plenty and success.

MEETING WITH DIFFICULTIES.

The second batch of emigrants also met with difficulties at the outset. Eighteen families enhanced their difficulties by refusing to take the lands chosen for them, and wandering afield to find others. The heads of some of these wandering families, making, after all, but a poor selection of lands, fell to the temptation of excellent wages in a distant lumber industry, and after a while deserted their holdings, and somehow found the means of transferring themselves and their families hundreds of miles to the wage-earning locality. Possibly they will return to their holdings, especially as all who remained are now doing well, and feeling more than contented; the very greatest original grumbler among them on first arrival declaring that now no power on earth shall drag him from his holding.

AT WORK IN CANADA.

These crofters have now built for themselves very comfortable houses; they own working oxen, milk cows, and even horses; they are accused of having bought more waggons and reapers and binders and other agricultural machines than they have need of; and, as I pointed out at the beginning of this article, the actual

Greetings from a group of Manitobans at Manitoba.

results of their labours are to place each family in a fair way to own a prosperous farm of 160 acres. Some live close by lakes and streams, affording plenty of good trout and wild fowl. Good school and kirk accommodation is already provided, and there can be no doubt but that in another three years these settlements will be among the most well-to-do of the prairie "locations." Lord Lothian is certainly to be congratulated upon the success of his experiment.

Mr Scarth, Dominion Member of Parliament for Winnipeg, took great personal trouble in the settling of these Highland crofters, and he and Mrs Scarth lived amongst them for the first few weeks, when they arrived as strangers, without friends, and had to be camped out in tents. He now kindly made all arrangements for us to visit the settlement, and I will give you a few extracts from my journal about our visit, written at the time, along with some pictures which tell their own tale :—

TUESDAY, October 7th, 1890.—Went to little hotel for breakfast, and by nine were ready for our start. Killarney rather a respectable little place for four years old. Mr Lalor, the local merchant, who has taken great charge of the Highland crofters whom we had come to see, had arranged to drive us at Mr Scarth's request. So off we went, A., Coutts, Mr Lalor, and myself, in what they call a "Democrat," a sort of long, four-wheeled cart, with two seats, one behind the other. It was a perfect day for our forty miles drive across the prairie; not much sun, but a bright shining always in the long fleecy clouds, which extend themselves in long, long stretches of manifold shapes in the way which we have come to look upon as especially Canadian. No wind, but an indescribably brisk bracing air, which we want to inhale in long breaths all the while. And, as we thought when travelling on a previous occasion in Texas and Dakota, driving on the prairie and on the trails running through the prairies is unlike any other driving. The soft elasticity of the ground carries one over all the bumps, and jars, and ruts; and roots and hillocks are all passed over as the most natural things in the world. But with all this, I am not going to rave about the scenery of Manitoba; for to a mountain bred visitor these everlasting prairies, with their serpentine black trails winding through them, appear, on first acquaintance at any rate, inexpressibly dreary.

Of course to-day we have been going through land but newly taken up, and there has not yet been time for the desire for beauty or comfort to grow. The struggle to live has naturally swallowed up all the energy of the settlers, and it has been quite the exception to see even any attempt after the commonest sort of tidiness, much less any effort to nurture a few flowers, a plant, or a tree. But the Manitobans have shown that they value education, for little schools are planted down everywhere where there are fifteen children to attend, and the teachers are not badly paid. We went into one of these schools to-day, where there are about twenty children, and a pleasent looking young man, an M.A., who also has a farm in the neighbourhood, was teaching them. He said the great difficulty was the irregularity of attendance, which made his work resemble that of Sisyphus and become real drudgery. Such country schools are shut up during the winter, and in the autumn the children are kept away for harvest work, so that it is only the three spring months that can be depended on.

Our first visit was to the old Irishman O'Brien, who constituted himself the god-father of the place, and insisted on its being called Killarney. I am afraid that my smothered exclamation of amusement on first sight of the lake, remembering our first sight of the real Killarney, was taken as disrespectful by our cicerone, but, in truth, it *is* the prettiest thing we have seen in Manitoba.

After seven or eight miles we came to the first crofter, one John Macleod, who had been one of the grumblers about small things, but he made no grumble to us, and said he thought he should get along well now. Then came John Nicholson's section. He is one of the most successful, but, unfortunately he and his wife were away from home. He had his ten acres cultivated according to stipulation the first year (1889), this year he had 55; next year he is preparing for 75. His wheat has been thrashed, and we saw it all in his new little wooden barn—900 bushels, representing about £150. His first barn was still standing, made of sods. Other four crofters to the West are relations, and all on one section, and are doing well. We saw two more of the Lewes families, John Campbell and his

Mr and Mrs Peter Graham's cottage.

wife and children, in whose cottage also was old Mrs Macleod, whose husband holds meetings while the missionary is away in the winter, Mrs Macdonald, Peter Graham and his wife, a tidy, capable-looking woman with five bonny bairns. We photographed some of the people and their places, though some were very unwilling, being in their working clothes. One requires to think of what these people were before they came out, to appreciate their present position and prospects. Some who came knew nothing about agircultural work—one had never used a hay-fork in his life. And that they should have got on so well as they have done is very

Mr and Mrs John Campbell's home.

creditable, both to themselves and their neighbours. After leaving the crofters we came in sight of Pelican Lake, and then, descending a steep brae, the sight of which rejoiced our hearts, we came upon a prosperous-looking farm, 640 acres, owned by a man whom we passed ploughing. We stopped to ask our way, but, after all got rather

Across the Prairies. 111

astray, and went a good bit out of our way up a rough hill, which landed us on the edge of a ravine, on the other side of which was the house where we were to have luncheon. A young English farmer of cheery and hopeful aspect, and newly married, put us right again, and we were then ready for our four o'clock luncheon, at Mrs Darough's, at the farmhouse of Glenfern. The threshing was going on there, and they had had a busy day, with 16 or 17 men

The Darough family at Glenfern.

in to dinner. The yield had not been so good as expected, and one field, from which they expected twenty-five bushels per acre, had only fifteen. They were doing better to-day. That same field in 1887 yielded 40 bushels per acre (sold at 48 cents), in 1888 it was down to five bushels per acre (sold at 84 cents) in 1887 I forgot what she told me the number of bushels were, but the price was 64 cents. The Daroughs came from Ontario, and are of Scotch extraction. There are five sons, three working, the eldest, just married to one of the crofter girls, living on a section of his own, and two daughters, who gave us proofs of their prowess in the homemade bread and jam and pumpkin pie. But Mrs Darough said that sugar had been too dear to make much jam. All the smaller kinds of fruit do well, and wild berries abound. Potatoes, cabbages, cauliflowers, and other vegetables grow magnificently. Apples are not yet a success. Coutts left us here, and we drove on to Glenboro, about 21 miles further, calling in at two of the Harris crofters *en route*, Morrison and Donald Stewart. Only saw the wife of the latter, who worked for Lord Dunmore until he sold the Island. Many messages sent to the Dunmores.

All the last part of the drive, which passes through rich wheat land and past a prosperous Scandinavian settlement, was lost on us, for it had become quite dark, and our attention was concentrated on our driver avoiding the many vehicles returning from Glenboro Fair—waggons, and carts, and buggies, and gigs, and droves of cattle and horses. He managed very creditably, and the demeanour of the home-going folk contrasted favourably with what might have been on some similar occasions at home.

IX.

IN A RAILWAY ACCIDENT.

IN the English newspapers of last October appeared telegraphic reports of a railway accident west of Winnipeg, finishing up with the statement that Lord and Lady Aberdeen were on the train, and that while the former went about ministering to the wants of the wounded, the latter took sketches of the scene. That was a tolerably hard-hearted proceeding, was it not? I wonder what those of our Members and Associates who happened to notice this statement thought of the doings of their President while she was away beyond their reach. Well, here is the true unvarnished statement of the facts, as written at the time:—

"We started from Winnipeg soon after six, and about eight we had just gone across to the dining-car and begun our dinner, when there came a sudden tremendous screwing on of the brakes, a series of jerks, an abrupt transference of crockery and glass from tables to floor, and then the car was motionless, and all was perfectly still. People looked at one another for a moment—the same unuttered thought passing through each mind,—then came the tidings, 'The engine is off the rails!' A. rushed off with others to see what had really occurred, and we were amazed to find how much damage was done, when we remembered the comparitively slight shock we had felt. The engine was lying on its side, on the bank, all crumpled and torn, the funnel half into the ground and still smoking away; the tender, upside down across the rails, towering above the luggage-van on its side. On the other side of the line, one car half down the bank, and three more off the rails; the three last cars, including the dining-car and ours, were still on the rails. No one could ascertain the cause of the accident, and for a few minutes there was great suspense as to whether any one was killed or injured. Marvellously and mercifully no one was killed, and the engine-driver, fire-man, and express messenger were only somewhat cut and bruised. The driver had, with great presence of mind, turned off steam, put on the brakes at the first jerk, and then jumped off; the fireman remained, thinking, as he himself expressed it, that the engine would "ride the ties." It is wonderful how he escaped, when the part of the engine where he was sitting was all smashed. All in the dark and by the light of a lantern held by A., I tried to make a sketch of the wreck, but it was so dark and drizzling that it was rather difficult work. It all looked very weird. The engine gave one the impression of a great, gasping, living thing, with its head buried in the earth, still hissing and steaming in impotent misery, and, to increase the mystery of the scene, dark figures flitted about here, there, and everywhere, with lanterns, and in the near distance there loomed a great threatening fiery eye, barring our way. This latter apparition turned out to be the lights of the engine of a freight train, which had been waiting at the next station (Poplar Point) till we should pass, and now came up to see what could be done. It was past twelve when we heard the tinkling bell announcing the arrival of the wreck-train 'with a break-down gang' from Winnipeg, (thirty-five miles away), with superintendent, doctor, and engineer aboard. We, from our post of vantage, at the end of the train, saw the lights

Scene of Accident, from a sketch made by Lady Aberdeen same night.

approach slowly and cautiously. A party from our train were on the outlook for them, and motioned them to proceed by swinging a lantern backwards and forwards, but they crept up inch by inch making sure of their way as they came. And then all at once the

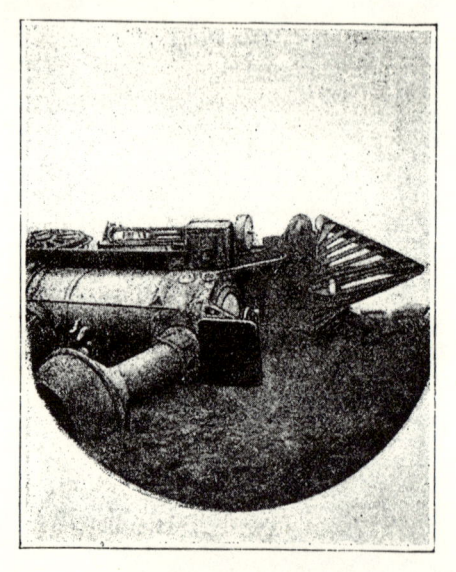

Our Engine as photographed by the Kadok the morning after accident.

place was alive with groups of the new-comers, surrounding the remains of our wrecked train, examining, enquiring, testing the amount of damage done, and ere long setting to work with pick-axe and spade to remove the *débris* which lay across the torn-up line. It was soon decided that the quickest method was to construct

In a Railway Accident. 117

a temporary new line for the few hundred yards or so which had been destroyed, and while this was being done, the uninjured cars were pulled back to Raeburn, the first station back.

Off again!

"*Oct. 10.*—By mid-day the line was in order for us to proceed, and a new engine was in readiness. We had already, however, walked forward to the scene of the disaster, having arranged with the conductor to be picked up by the train as it came up. We tried some photos. But the weather was very dark for that. It was only now that we ascertained the cause of our accident, *i.e.*, a drove of cattle, which in the pitchy black night, were not perceived. A big ox was killed, and two poor cows got their legs broken. Is it not wonderful how animals suffer in silence? Fancy our not hearing a sound from these poor beasts under the train when we were standing about! They were not discovered till the men set to work. The next day as we passed, the poor cows were lying piteously on the bank, with such a scared look in their eyes, and making miserable attempts to rise. The railway people dared not put an end to their sufferings, lest their owners should bring an action for damages—and the owners, although they had been notified of the accident had not yet appeared on the scene."

It is wonderful how such accidents do not occur oftener on dark nights, when the train is passing along such vast stretches of unfenced land, over which cattle roam at their own free will. As it happened, there *were* fences on either side of the line at this particular spot, so the cattle must have strayed in by some open gate, and were doubtless lying on the track because of its comparative dryness after the deluge of rain that had been coming down. You will notice in the illustration of the fallen engine the iron pointed contrivance in front invented on purpose to guard against such mishaps. It is called the "cow-catcher," and is intended to sweep any animal off the line that may be bent on self-

In a Railway Accident

destruction. Our accident, however, proves that it is not always successful in its purpose, but I should add that accidents on the C.P.R. have hitherto happily been exceedingly rare, owing to the constant and vigilant care of those in charge of the line, and who arrange perpetual supervision of every part of the track, so that all possible danger may be averted.

The "cow-catcher" in front of the engine has sometimes been put to another and original use at times. Adventurous travellers have obtained permission to sit on it whilst travelling through the magnificent scenery on the route of the C.P.R., in order to obtain the best possible views of all that is to be seen from the line. You would not imagine such a position very comfortable, would you? But those who have tried it speak of their experiences with enthusiasm. Amongst others, Lady Macdonald, the wife of the late Premier of Canada, took a trip West on the "cow-catcher," of which she has written a charming account. We were not so bold, and contented ourselves with the outlook from our car, and this for two or three days after leaving Winnipeg consisted solely in vast stretches, which the poet Bryant describes as—

> The gardens of the Desert, these.
> The unshorn fields, boundless and beautiful,
> For which the speech of England has no name—
> The Prairies. I behold them for the first,
> And my heart swells, while the dilated sight

Takes in the encircling vastness.   Lo ! they lie
In airy undulations, far away,
As if the ocean, in his gentlest swell,
Stood still, with all his rounded billows fixed
And motionless for ever.—Motionless?
No—they are all unchained again.   The clouds
Sweep over with their shadows, and beneath
The surface rolls and fluctuates to the eye.
Man hath no part in all this glorious work :
The hand that built the firmament hath heaved
And smoothed these verdant swells, and sown their slopes,
With herbage. . . .   The great heavens
Seem to stoop down upon the scene in love,—
A nearer vault, and of a tender blue,
Than that which bends above the eastern hills. . . .
In these plains the bison feeds no more, where once he shook
The earth with thundering steps—yet here I meet
His ancient footprints stamped beside the pool.
Still this great solitude is quick with life,
Myriads of insects, gaudy as the flowers
They flutter over, gentle quadrupeds,
And birds, that scarce have learned the fear of man,
Are here, and sliding reptiles of the ground,
Startling beautiful. . . .   The bee,
A more adventurous colonist than man,
With whom he comes across the eastern deep,
Fills the savannas with his murmurings,
And hides his sweets, as in the olden age,
Within the hollow oak.   I listen long
To his domestic hum, and think I hear .
The sound of that advancing multitude

> Which soon shall fill these deserts. From the ground
> Comes up the laugh of children, the soft voice
> Of maidens, and the sweet and solemn hymn
> Of Sabbath worshippers. The low of herds
> Bends with the rustling of the heavy grain
> Over the dark-brown furrows. All at once
> A fresher wind sweeps by, and breaks my dream.
> And I am in the wilderness alone.

Alone! Yes, I think that settlers on the prairie must realise what solitude means in a way which can scarcely be understood by those living in mountainous regions. The mountains and tree-clad crags seem to encircle and protect those who dwell among them with so real and living a personality that these can never feel "alone" in their company. But go to the prairie country and look around—you may see the bright colours of butterfly and flower, you may smile at the cunning looks of the little rabbit-like sort of creatures called "prairie dogs," who rear themselves up on their hind legs and look at you, and then "*heigh, presto,*" they are off; you may hear the rushing through the air of the flocks of wild geese overhead, on their way to their winter quarters, but of human habitation you will see but scant signs. Your eye may scan many square miles around, and yet you may scarcely be able to detect any indication of the fact that the lords of this rich harvest land are beginning to enter upon their inheritance. Yet it is so. And if we had paid our Western visit during harvest-time, we should have seen some such sights as you see represented in the accompanying pictures. When you are reading this, we shall be hearing rejoicing accounts of the bounteousness of the harvest which farmers in Manitoba and the North-West have been gathering in this year without any

A regiment of workers on the Prairie.

damage from the dreaded early frosts. And I shall be trying to grow wise as to the reasons why the Manitoban black mud, which lies from two to four feet in depth on the surface of the soil, is so rich as to produce magnificent crops without manure. Once more, too, it will be impressed on us that the settlers who do best are those who adapt themselves most to the methods of farming found successful in the new country. For instance, they must not plough deep as they do at home, but only about two inches, and then they must put in a crop at the first breaking, as this has been found the best way of subduing the sod, besides the advantage of yielding profit to the farmer the first year, when his means are not generally plentiful. This sod is very hard to break at first, but subsequent ploughings are easy. As we went along, we found one and another of our fellow-passengers quite willing to tell us about all these things, and to explain the reasons as to why one man fails and the other succeeds. It was especially interesting to us to come across young men, from our own district in Aberdeenshire, who could speak in cheery tones of their past experience and their future prospects. One of these, Mr Will, from Methlick, who came and chatted with us on our car for a bit, had been working for a year or two on one of the huge 10,000 acre farms, formed originally by Sir John Lister-Kaye; when we met him, he was about to buy a farm of his own, and to bring to it as mistress an Associate of the "Onward and Upward Association." But death broke up his home only a few months later, and he is now foreman on Lord Aberdeen's estate in British Columbia.

This young man's experience, and that of others whom we met, points to the fact that one of the best ways of getting on is for a new comer to hire himself as labourer to a good farmer for a year or two, so as not only to save up money for his start, but also, even if he have some capital, to learn the ways of the country under practical guidance. In looking to the future and to the pro-

One of Sir John Lister-Kaye's big farms in Alberta.

bability of the continuance of the rich crops which have been obtained these last few years from Manitoba and the North - West, there is one encouraging feature which was brought before us by a gentleman at Ottawa, Mr Hurlbert, who has prepared a series of very interest-

Passing a car-full of emigrants—" Take our pictures."

ing maps under the sanction of the Canadian Government. One of these maps, part of which we have reproduced here on a small scale, shows us that all over the world there are

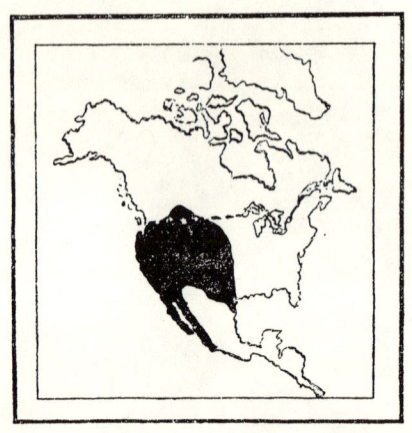

Map showing region of summer droughts in North America.

regions where summer droughts prevail, where rain falls but rarely during the period while the crops are growing and requiring moisture. If you look at the map, you will see that but a small part of this region is included in the Dominion of Canada, and this is a matter of no small importance to intending settlers.

As we get further West, we begin to hear about other sources of prosperity besides wheat—we hear of the grass lands of Alberta, and its openings for large ranches for the breeding of horses; we hear, too, of coal-fields of

In a Railway Accident. 127

such extent that all past fears as to the fuel resources of Canada have been set at rest. Then, too, there is the timber, and large petroleum deposits. But I cannot enlarge on these things in this paper, nor will I describe to you the young towns of this region : Regina, the capital of the

A horse ranch near Calgary.

North-West, where too are the head-quarters of the smart red-uniformed Canadian Mounted Police ; Medicine Hat, a little town in a cavity, surrounded by strongly indented hills, where we had the pleasure of inspecting a charmingly-appointed hospital, erected through the efforts of

Mr Niblock, one of the C.P.R. Superintendents; and Calgary, at the foot of the Rockies, a rapidly rising town which seems likely to become an important centre.

If space had permitted, I would have wished to tell you something of the former masters of this country, the Indians, who are diminishing in numbers, and will ere long disappear. Their tents, or "teepees," are pitched in groups on the plains you pass by, and miserable specimens in dirty squalid-coloured blankets haunt the railway stations, with the object of selling buffalo horns, or baskets, or feather-work. Their babies, whom they call "papooses," and who are strapped to boards which their mothers carry on their backs, seem to be model babies. You never hear one crying. There they are, swathed up tightly on their boards, and they appear to be equally unconcerned if they are riding on their mothers' backs, or are put down against a wall, whilst their guardians are otherwise occupied. But travellers who pass through these countries only by the railway can know nothing of the lives and customs of the true type of Indian. For knowledge of these we must go to the hunter, the Hudson's Bay Company trader, and the missionary, and we must hunt records of the past, which already have supplied material for tales of thrilling adventure to the writers of boys' books.

When the Europeans came to America, all this vast region, of which we have been speaking, was only inhabited by various tribes of Indians, who lived almost entirely on the proceeds of their fishing and hunting. Gradually the white men came to realise what a source of wealth existed in the herds of fur-covered animals which roamed over these endless plains and mountains, and the skins of which could be obtained very easily from the Indians for a few beads, ornaments, or better still, for muskets when they had learned how to use them, or for the spirits, which were to work such havoc among the native races. And in 1669 Prince Rupert formed a Company, which was endowed by King Charles II., with "all countries which lie within the entrance of Hudson's Straits, in whatever latitude they may be, so far as not possessed by other Christian States." The new Company entered vigorously on its work, establishing central trading stations throughout their domain, formed of a few wooden huts, and surrounded by palisades or walls and well-barred gates. These were generally near rivers, and to these the savages brought their merchandise of skins, and feathers, and horns, at stated seasons of the year. They encamped before the fort, and a solemn transaction, of bartering and of affectionate speeches, took place, and on the results of this bartering the Company grew fabulously rich. A century later their continued success caused another Company to be formed, and many were the feuds which ensued, until the two decided to unite and to work together. Oh, the yarns that might be told of those golden days of hunting, of the adventures and hairbreadth escapes, and in all the Red Man plays a conspicuous part. Round his loyalty or his enmity centres many a tale. Those days are over now. In 1869 the Government took over the domains of the Hudson's Bay Company for £300,000, and certain lands round the trading stations, and from that time the era of the Indian was over. They cannot stand before the forces of civilisation, and they are doomed to give way to those who have entered on their predestined work of cultivating the land and building cities, thus multiplying the population and replenishing the earth. Meanwhile, the missionaries have been busy. The authorities of the Hudson's Bay Company always encouraged their efforts, and did much for them by forbidding the use of spirits at their stations, and in later times the Government has endeavoured to exercise a paternal care over these perishing tribes, gathering them into reserves, trying to teach them agriculture, educating their children, granting gifts and pensions, and doing all in their power to promote the success of the Missions. But of the heroic work of these missionaries, and of what they have been able to accomplish, we must tell you some other time, if you will not tire of the subject.

X.

THE ROCKY MOUNTAINS.

AND now we have come to the last part of the trip through which I have endeavoured to act as your conductor. And if I have felt myself inefficient in that capacity during the earlier parts of our journey, still more do I feel the impossibility of doing justice to all the glories of the scenery through which we shall now pass. For even the prairies of the North West prove themselves to be not so limitless as they appear at first to those traversing their vast extent day after day; and one night, as we peep out of our berths behind the closed blinds of the car, we find ourselves standing still at the very foot of the Rockies. In the conflicting light of the stars and early dawn, we see ourselves guarded by three high purple peaks, known as the Three Sisters, and we feel ourselves once more safe at home in the bosom of the mountains. Soon the heavy engine which is to pant up the steep inclines in front of us comes, and hooks us on, and all day long, as we clamber the snow-covered Rockies, and steam on slowly through the heart of the Selkirks, along the Columbia River, and the wild waters which sweep down the Kicking-Horse Pass, and pass under the shade of the crags of huge "Sir Donald," we rush about from side to side, and from end to end of our car, attempting, if not to photograph or sketch, at least to imprint some memory of the magnificent panorama unrolling itself before our eyes. But all in vain! There is such a thing as being surfeited with fine scenery, and it

Approaching the Rockies.

is a transgression against nature to hurry, as we did through these glorious scenes. All that remains now is a remembrance of towering snow-capped peaks rearing themselves up in all their strength above us, and stretches of mountains changing in the varying light of sun and cloud, from palest blues and greys to rich tones of yellow

"The Three Sisters."

and red and purple, as we come nearer, and as the autumn foliage shows itself blending with the deep browns and blueish-green colours of the waters foaming below. To appreciate scenery such as this frequent halts should be made, and time should be allowed for the eye and mind to drink in and realise what is before them. Solitude too, and deep, unbroken stillness, are needed, if you would be in harmony with these surroundings, if you would have nature lead you up irresistibly to nature's God, if you would be able from your heart to bow yourself down and say :—

> "These are Thy glorious works, Parent of good,
> Almighty, Thine this universal frame,
> Thus wondrous fair ! Thyself how wondrous then !
> Unspeakable ! who sits above these heavens
> To us invisible, or dimly seen
> In these Thy lowest works, yet these
> Declare Thy goodness beyond thought
> And power divine."

Another time we hope to be able to stop at various places on this route, for a day at any rate, and perhaps I shall thus be better fitted to be your guide on some future occasion. The only halt we did make in these regions we enjoyed immensely. It was at Banff, where the Government are forming a National Park, twenty-six miles long by ten broad, and where the C.P.R. have put up a most comfortable hotel, 4000 feet above the sea, overlooking the Bow River. The hotel is about one and

The Rocky Mountains. 135

a half miles from the station. Our train arrived at the station about 1 A.M., and we shall not soon forget the brisk drive in the bright, frosty air, over snow-besprinkled grounds, amidst snow-covered mountains, with stars glimmering overhead. The hotel is a prettily-designed

From the window of the Banff Hotel.

wooden building, capable of accommodating a hundred guests, and in the large entrance-hall a huge log-fire, crackling away on an open hearth, bids welcome to weary travellers from East and West, whatever hour of the night they may arrive. Well, we had what is termed in America "a lovely time" at Banff. The sun shone brilliantly, the air was exhilarating, and we made the

Cascade Mountain, Banff

most of our one day. We walked, and we sketched, and we "kodaked"—we visited the hot sulphur springs, which are much resorted to by invalids, and which boil out of the ground at different degrees of temperature up to 90 or 92 degrees. Some of these look most tempting to the bather, the clear green-blue water bubbling into a large pool, enclosed by high rocks, and the rays of the sun glinting through the opening above. And in the afternoon Captain Harper, one of the Inspectors of the Mounted Police, came round with his break and four-in-hand, and took us for a drive round the Park, charioteering us most skilfully up and down the steep roads, winding round Tunnel Mountain, and showing us many beautiful views.

The time for departure came all too soon, and as we were standing near the station in the darkness, waiting for the arrival of the train, I heard a familiar Aberdeenshire voice putting the question, "Do you remember "Titaboutie?" "Remember Titaboutie!" I should think we did! The voice belonged to a daughter of one of Lord Aberdeen's Tarland tenants, and we found that she and her sister had both come out to Canada. One was engaged at the Banff Sanatorium, the other was with her brother on one of Sir John Lister-Kaye's farms, and both said they liked the country. It was a touch of home where we had least expected it, but it was by no means a solitary experience. Wherever we went, it seemed as if we met " oor ain folk," and these same folk seem generally to get " the guiding o't." That reflection should do more than fill our hearts with pride of old Scotland, it should bring home to those of us who are parents the additional responsibility of being parents of children who belong to a race who seemed bound to rise to high position and influence wherever they may go, the world over. The thought that the destinies of countries far away may one day largely rest in our children's hands should fill us with a noble ambition for them, that they may be able to say with others who have gone before —

> " We cross the prairie as of old
> The pilgrims crossed the sea,
> To make the West, as they the East,
> The homestead of the free.
>
> " We go to plant her common schools
> On distant prairie swells,
> And give the Sabbaths of the wilds
> The music of her bells.
>
> " Upbearing, like the ark of old,
> The Bible in our van,
> We go to test the truth of God,
> Against the foes of man."

Undoubtedly Scotchmen have largely had to do with the making of Canada, and happily they have for the most part left their mark on her for good. We find their names much associated too with the making of this

The Van Horne Range—sketched from Field.

wonderful railway, by means of which all this marvellous scenery is witnessed. If we think of what was considered a good road in these parts before the railway came, and then when we travel by this iron road cut through, or cut out of the sides of, perpendicular cliffs, the workmen

A Trestle Bridge.

in some cases having had to be lowered by ropes from above in order to get at their work, we get some idea of the change which has been wrought. From side to side of rushing waters the train crosses on trestle bridges like that of which we give you an illustration, and finds its way along ledges of rock, twisting and turning in every

The Rocky Mountains. 141

direction on the brink of the precipices below. On some parts of the road great wooden erections, called snow-sheds (having something of the character of tunnels), have had to be put up to protect the line from snow in winter. By this means the road is scarcely, if ever, blocked, even during heavy falls of snow. And thus, by one device and another, and by the exercise of constant, vigilant inspection, this railway company, though their system covers such an extent of country, and has to face so many perilous places, can, up to the present time, thankfully record that they have only lost the life of one passenger, and that was in consequence of his standing on the steps of the car after being warned by the conductor not to do so.

I could tell you much of the glimpses we caught of life in British Columbia, of the Indians spearing the salmon, of the Chinamen washing the sand for gold, of the villages of both Indians and Chinese, which are quite different to any other we have seen, and the curious burying-places, high up in the trees, which the Indians make for their dead But I prefer to wait until I have seen more of all this, and will then gladly give you a paper or two, exclusively on British Columbia, if you should wish it.

I will only ask you on this occasion to come straight on to the cities of Vancouver and Victoria, and take a look of these before we part.

At Vancouver we were most hospitably entertained by

the Mayor, Mr Oppenheimer, and his wife, and, in addition to this, the Scotch and the Irish residents combined together to give us a most hearty and kindly reception one evening. In this way we heard much of all that was doing in the place, and of its wonderful

Vancouver.

growth since the disastrous fire which utterely annihilated it five years ago. Within three months after the fire four hundred houses had been erected, and the progress has since been so rapid that there is now a population of 13,000. This is the more remarkable when we reflect that the site on which the town stands was covered with a dense forest, of enormous pines, such as we now see just outside the limits of present habitations. Their great roots have to be removed, and the heavy wood and dead timber have to be cleared at an enormous expense before the land can be utilised, yet a great part of this forest is already parcelled out into building blocks, and is selling

The late Mr G. G. Mackay.

at a high price. And where the Douglas pine and the cedar flourished undisturbed but a few years ago, handsome streets are now formed, lighted with electric light, and supplied with electric tram-cars. Most of the buildings are of wood, but there are a few principal streets where only stone or brick buildings may be erected. Great foresight is also being shown by the municipal authorities in matters of sanitation and drainage, unlike some new towns, where such matters have been left to chance; and even in these early days a Public Park has been set aside, with a circuit of ten miles, called after the present Governor-General, the Stanley Park.

We had the advantage of being shown some of the country round Vancouver by an old friend (Mr G. G. Mackay) whom I have often seen during my childhood at my father's home in Inverness-shire. He came out here three years ago to see if this would be a good place for his sons, and liked it so much that he never went back, but sent for his family to join him. As he pointed out to us, the peninsula on which Vancouver is situated on either side of her beautiful harbour is bound to be built over, and to become exceedingly valuable, as the city develops under the increase of trade which must of necessity come, through its being the terminus of the C.P.R., and commanding the shortest route to Japan, China, and India, by the new magnificent steam-ships which are now running. Just ten weeks ago, the advantage of this route over any other was demonstrated by the Japanese mail reaching Queenstown in twenty days from leaving Yokohama. You may imagine the pride of the Vancouver people at seeing "The Empress of Japan" sail proudly in after a nine day's voyage from Yokohama.

The atmosphere of hope and faith in the future of their

country make British Columbians a very delightful people. There is a spirit of enterprise in the air which, coupled to natural advantages, makes success a certainty. This belief in the future was rather amusingly illustrated by a huge sign-board which we found stuck into the ground, on the borders of a dense forest with no house in sight. The notice ran thus:—

> " There is a tide in the affairs of men,
> Which, taken at its flood, leads on to fortune !
> *This* is the tide of *your life ! !*
> *Invest* in the city of the future, *Steveston*,
> And become
> A MILLIONAIRE."

I wonder whether we shall find the city of Steveston an accomplished fact this year?

We must tear ourselves away from Vancouver and its beautiful surroundings with regret, and embark in the "Islander" for the five hours' crossing to Victoria, under Captain Hulden's care. See Mount Baker raising its head high above the sunset clouds, all in a golden glory, and seeming isolated far above all the rest of the common world below. And there, opposite, are the peaks of the famed Olympic Range, standing out a deep blue against the sky, only hidden here and there by a light mist curling about their sides. So we sail out of Vancouver, and the sunset fades into moonlight over a delightfully calm sea long before we reach Victoria, the beautiful capital of

British Columbia. Is it indeed Victoria and Vancouver Island where we have arrived? Has not the "Islander" lost her way, and brought us by a short route back to England, and landed at Torquay? The resemblance has almost a touch of the comical in it—the same scents, the same sort of greenness all round, the same sort of ferns and foliage and surroundings, and on that day, at

His Honour the Lieut.-Governor of British Columbia.

any rate, the same moist feeling in the air, developing later on into a steady downpour. Then English voices and faces abound, and English customs predominate so largely that the illusion would be complete if we were not recalled to our whereabouts by the presence of the Chinese pigtail everywhere.

The residents of British Columbia would be hard put

to it if it were not for these same Chinese. Domestic servants are very difficult to get, and even when obtained often give themselves such airs that the mistresses are glad to return to the Chinaman, who will act as cook, housemaid, waiter, groom, and gardener, all in one, without giving any trouble. Girls, however, who do come out, and are ready to work and do what they are told, get

Admiral Hotham.

very high wages. Labour generally is very dear. An ordinary labourer will get 10s. to 12s. a day, and mechanics and masons get as much as 16s. to 20s. a day.

We much regretted that the steady rain prevented us from seeing all the beauties of the place. But the Governor of British Columbia, and Mrs Nelson, and Sir Joseph and Lady Trutch, were ready to help us to see all that could be seen. The Governor kindly drove us down to the magnificent harbour at Esquimault, three miles from Victoria, the headquarters of the North Pacific Squadron. Several warships were riding at anchor, adding one more touch to the likeness to England. The Admiral

H.M.S. "Warspite."

of the Fleet, Admiral Hotham, had been good enough to give us an invitation to tea on board the flagship, the "Warspite," commanded by Captain Hedworth Lambton, and so here, on the Pacific Ocean, I paid my first visit to a British war-ship. Everything on board looked spotless in its whiteness, and brightness, and trimness, and the Admiral's room, in the end bows of the ship, was like a drawing-room for cosiness and comfort—a bright fire burning in a grate, and comfortable chairs and tables and ornaments, all looking as if we were ashore. Admiral Hotham gave a high character to British Columbia; he had been here for five months, and this was only the second wet day he had seen—climate, people, and all surroundings were amongst the pleasantest he had known in all his nautical wanderings. It was sad that we should not have the opportunity of seeing the place to full advantage, but our brief stay was full of enjoyments, including an evening at Government House; and here, too, we met our friend, Professor Henry Drummond, who had just arrived from Australia and Japan, and who now joined our party for the homeward trip.

Here, then, amidst the roses and fragrant breezes of this favoured isle, I must leave you, with many regrets that our trip has come to an end. It is a hurried journey that we have taken, and we have had but glimpses of the inexhaustable resources of this great country. But if these little sketches have added somewhat to your knowledge of what Canada is, if it has increased your pride in her, if it has kindled a desire to do what may be in your power to build up her fortunes, I shall feel they have not been written in vain. The high moral and religious character of her present populations, the wise and true foundations that they are laying for future development and prosperity, makes one long that those remaining in the old country should thoroughly realise how much reason they have to rejoice in our common kinship, and that those thinking of coming out to Canada to try their fortunes should come with a hearty desire to do their utmost for the land of their adoption. There has been some disappointment this year at the increase of the population during the last decade being only half a million. Still all admit that the settlers are of a good stamp, and this, after all, is of far more importance than mere numbers. Strong in her sense of her future, she can afford to wait. As we sail down her rivers and lakes, and traverse her prairies, and climb her mountains, the poet Whittier's words haunt us—

> " I hear the tread of pioneers,
> Of nations yet to be,
> The first low wash of waves where soon
> Shall roll a human sea."

Our eyes may not see this consummation, but we may join our prayers to those of a Canadian poet, with whose words I will close:—

> " Canada ! Maple-land ! Land of great mountains !
> Lake-land and river-land ! Land 'twixt the seas !
> Grant us, God, hearts that are large as our heritage,
> Spirits as free as the breeze !

"Grant us Thy fear, that we may walk in humility,—
 Fear that is rev'rent, not fear that is base:—
Grant to us righteousness, wisdom, prosperity,
 Peace—if unstained by disgrace.

"Grant us Thy love, and the love of our country!
 Grant us Thy strength, for our strength's in Thy name;
Shield us from danger, from every adversity,
 Shield us, O Father, from shame.

"Last born of nations! The offspring of freedom!
 Heir to wide prairies, thick forests, red gold!
God grant us wisdom to value our birthright,
 Courage to guard what we own."

Lord Aberdeen and Professor H. Drummond in the Railway Car.

XI.

A VISIT TO BRITISH COLUMBIA

1892

EN ROUTE TO GUISACHAN, B.C.

THE very mention of the place is restful and delightful! Never have we had such a holiday anywhere, and even now a mere allusion to "Guisachan, B.C.," is sufficient to produce a soothing sensation in the minds of the trio of holiday-makers whose visit I want to describe. But how to approach the subject in a calm and judicial spirit! There's the rub! Our feelings regarding the place are betrayed already, and how am I to convince you that I am a trustworthy reporter? Well, I must just let facts speak for themselves; and now to begin at the very beginning!

How did we get there? Perhaps some of you may remember in our travels last year, "Through Canada with a Kodak," a day's halt at fair Canadian "Banff," nestling under the shade of the mighty Rockies, and yearly attracting to its magnificent solitudes an increasing number of seekers after change, and rest, and health. The remembrance of our former experience led us to make this again a resting-place, and much might be said concerning the walks and drives, and exploring rambles taken, and the friendships made, during the ten days which we spent peacefully in the midst of the everlasting hills, enjoying the most exquisite sunshiny weather all the while. But on this occasion I must content myself by merely referring to it as the place from which we started for our journey to our British Columbian home.

Early in the morning the West-bound train, bearing the traces of a prairie blizzard of hail and snow, through which it had passed, but which we had escaped, picked up our private car, whither we had repaired over night. All day long we had the delight of passing afresh through the scenes of beauty and grandeur which had so fascinated us on our previous trip. A brilliant sun lighted up the snow-capped peaks, the shining glaciers, and the foaming torrents, and melted away at last in a fiery glow of glory. Evening found us arrived at Sicamous Junction, where we were to spend the night, and where we were to leave the main-line, and to wend our way southwards along a track in course of construction to our valley of the Okanagan. Sicamous, situated on the

Guisachan Farm.   155

lovely Shushwap Lake, noted for its fine fishing, already boasts of a good-sized hotel, although but few other dwellings are to be seen. We had arrived in time to travel by the first passenger train along the new line. As mentioned, it was only now in course of construction, and only half of the fifty miles between Sicamous and Vernon, our county town, were completed. The railway authorities, however, complied with Lord Aberdeen's request for a special train which he chartered for the occasion. As it happened, Vernon was to hold her first Agricultural Show on this very day ; and, in consequence of this, a number of other passengers desired conveyance, and they were glad to get the chance of a train instead of making the trip in one of the hand-cars used by the workmen on the railway. These are worked by means of a pump-like contrivance, and doubtless look very cheery little vehicles. Let me own that a difference of opinion exists amongst our own party as to the charms of riding on these hand-cars. Lord Aberdeen is enthusiastic in their praise, whereas his wife is inclined to prefer her own feet as a means of locomotion to whizzing through the air at the rate of 20 miles an hour, when a choice must be made, and our little ten-year-old daughter—who formed the third of our travelling party—inclined to the opinion of one parent or the other in this matter, according to circumstances.

The first passenger train up the line was an event   It

consisted of an engine and tender, our private car (lent us through the kindness of Mr Spencer, of the C.P.R.), a "caboose," which I think may be described as a glorified guard's van, and two luggage trucks, on the top of which travelled a medley of men, dogs, packages, trunks, agricultural machinery, and all sorts of etceteras. We were all much interested in our own appearance, and we all got out at every halting-place, and surveyed ourselves with mingled pride and curiosity. At one of these temporary stations where we stopped to water the engine, by means of a very primitive wooden contrivance, we found quite an orchard and nursery-garden right alongside of the track. We were not surprised that the owner, Mr Thomson, was a Scotchman, nor that his wife was an "Ironside" from the Haddo House estates, so accustomed had we become to such coincidences; but these things being so, we were more than usually interested in hearing of what a good thing they were making of their 75 acres, what splendid fruit and vegetables could be produced in that district, and how they kept cows too, and poultry, getting 50 cents. (about 2s) per dozen eggs, and 50 cents. per spring chicken. A great part of our journey lay through very pretty country, skirting the Mara Lake, through picturesque mountain and wood scenery, after leaving Vernon, and then coming on the Spallumcheen River, along which a passenger steamer plies to Enderby, half-way to Vernon. After Enderby our driver had to

The first passenger train on the Shushwap and Okanagan Line halting at Enderby

take us cautiously, and often at foot's-pace, and even in this way we bumped and plunged strangely over the half-finished line, on which large gangs of workmen, mostly Chinese, were still working. But at last Vernon was reached without any mishap. The new little town of wooden houses, but already possessing four hotels and a fifth large one in course of erection, was evidently the scene of unwonted bustle. Little groups of eager agriculturists were discussing the prospects of the district, and their own individual fortunes; here and there waggons were unloading, buggies being unyoked, horses being led about in ribbons and exhibition apparel. The Commissioner of Lands and Works for the Province, the Hon. F. G. Vernon, after whom the town was named, was expected to open the Exhibition, but he not appearing, Lord Aberdeen was taken possession of by the Chairman, Mr Lumby, and the Committee, and the well-known process of inspecting the show and of making and hearing speeches was gone through with apparent satisfaction to all concerned. I say the process was a well-known one, but never at home have we had the pleasure of seeing such fruit, such roots, such vegetables. I wish I could give you some idea of the enormous size of the monster cabbages, of the melons and golden pumpkins, some of the former weighing as much as 30 and 40 lbs. The apples made a splendid show, as did also the pears, cherries, and all smaller fruits. Guisachan Farm did well, for it carried off six first prizes and six seconds.

Mr Lequime's little steamer which took us up the Lake to Guisachan.

Up to now but little attention has been devoted to fruit-growing, as this has been principally a stock-raising country, but the possibilities shown by the few orchards

Transferring the luggage from the train to the steamer.

already planted point to its being found to possess exceptional advantages for the pursuit of this industry.

While at the show we heard many desires expressed that the large ranche-owners in the neighbourhood could be persuaded to break up some of their property into fruit-farms from 20 to 100 acres, and it is because of this that Lord Aberdeen has now asked Mr G. G. Mackay, of Vancouver, to parcel out some of the property he has since acquired near Vernon into portions suitable for fruit-growing, and, at the same time, has arranged for the erection of a jam-factory. But more of this hereafter. Suffice it to say for the present, that great eagerness is being manifested on the subject by the inhabitants of the valley, and that a prosperous future is predicted for it by experienced judges, who point out not only the capabilities of production, but also the inexhaustible market existing in the North-West Provinces, where fruit cannot be grown to any advantage, and where there is a constantly growing demand for it.

But we must not linger at Vernon, though we were treated there with great kindness, and made many new friends. Especially do we remember the courtesy of Mr Dewdney, the Government agent, whose sad death since then has evoked such sincere sorrow and deep sympathy with his wife and family. We made acquaintance, too, with the pioneer settler of these parts, Mr Girouard, a French Canadian, who arrived here in 1858, having taken the best part of a year to travel hither from California, and with Mr Stuart, the enterprising young editor of the

Vernon News, a capital local paper, which brings us all the news of the district every week. But the day was wearing away, and my brother, who takes charge of Guisachan, was anxious that we should start on the final

Entrance Gate to Guisachan Farm.

stage of our journey. So we left the showyard before the judging of the cattle and horses was completed, but not before seeing a Guisachan team given a first prize, and another pair of useful horses

Guisachan Farm. 163

(which Lord A. had just purchased, on my brother

In the woods of Guisachan, B.C.

telling him that such a pair were needed on the

farm) gaining the same honourable position in another class.

The day was a general holiday, and the men who work the steamboat which carries passengers up and down the Okanagan Lake were away from work. In this emergency a neighbour of ours at Guisachan, Mr Lequime, undertook to take us home in his small steamboat. It was not intended exactly for passengers, but we had a very merry voyage, stowed away most of the time in a queer little cabin, father and daughter beguiling themselves and their companions by singing improvised Canadian railway songs to Scotch tunes. Presently the moon came out, and we had an opportunity of reconnoitring our Okanagan Lake beauties by moonlight. The time soon sped away, and ere four hours had passed we found ourselves turning into a bay, and presently we and our baggage were deposited on a landing stage, whilst our crew were hieing back to Vernon for an all-night ball in honour of the Show. They did not leave us, however, without securing a cart from a neighbour for our luggage, whilst we walked leisurely on to take possession of our new domain, only two miles distant. The telegram we had sent announcing the exact day of our arrival had never been received, and hence we had all the fun of appearing unexpectedly, and of a moonlight walk. Now, knowing that the beauty of a country is often over-rated, we had schooled ourselves not to expect much, so as not to be disappointed. We

View from the front door of Guisachan.

imagined to ourselves, therefore, a flat plain with bare hills in the distance, a few scrubby trees and bushes here and there, and a house set down in the middle of the flat. Instead of which we found mountains looking more like the Inverness-shire mountains of my youth than any others we had seen in Canada, and about a mile from the landing-stage we came to a gate leading into a wood. "Oh,

Guisachan, B.C.

if only that were our gate!" murmured Lord Aberdeen. "But that's just what it is," answered Coutts, my brother, and we turned into a regular delightful wood, with big trees of two hundred feet high, through which the moonlight fell in silvery streaks across the new road which my brother and his assistant-manager, Mr Smith, had prepared for us as a surprise. About half-a-mile brings us through the wood, and then, on emerging, we see our house a quarter of a mile away, standing against a background of purple hills, and commanding a charming view, with a peep of the lake from the verandah. On approaching our habitation it looked very much deserted and locked up, but Coutts knocked away in confidence that someone would appear. Presently a cautious step was heard within, and the door was presently opened a chink, and we were demanded what we wanted. It was perhaps as well for us that Coutts was with us, for Mr Smith afterwards owned that he had been very suspicious of us when he heard footsteps on the verandah, and he had loaded and brought his rifle with him behind the door, to repel us by force if need be, and the dogs "Cæsar" and "Spot" were quite ready to join in the chase until they heard the voice of their master assuring them that we were friends.

A warm reception—was it not? But we all agreed that we could not have had a more delightful home-coming than that moonlight walk with all its surprises, and then the storming of the citadel was much more in keeping with our mood than finding everybody and everything in readiness.

It took but a few minutes, however, to light up the house, and to show how ship-shape everything had been made to receive us, and we barely had time to examine all the ingenuities and tastefulness of the two bachelors in the household arrangements, when it was announced that "Foo," the Chinese cook and servant-in-general, had not only been roused out of his slumbers, but had prepared a substantial supper wherewith to appease our hunger. And soon thereafter we were all in the land of dreams, dreaming of delights, past, present, and future.

XII.

GUISACHAN FARM.

"WILL you come out for a bear hunt this afternoon?" That was the first communication which we received from the outer world the morning after our arrival at Guisachan. Two of our neighbours, hearing of our advent, had come up to say that a bear with her two cubs, had been seen coming down from the hills to search for the berries which were scarce last year higher up, and their present whereabouts being ascertained, it was proposed that they should pay for their temerity with their lives. Perhaps you will think that such an expedition does not sound like a very proper beginning for a respectable farmer and his family to make to his farming life in British Columbia. But truth will out, and the invitation was accepted and acted upon before we had ridden the marches or examined the stock. A beautiful day it was, too, for a hunt or an expedition of any kind! A quiet, gray morning, with light soft fleecy white clouds floating about the mountain tops, had brightened out into an afternoon full of sunshine, and we saw the surroundings of our new home under the most favourable auspices, as we trotted merrily over the fields, and through the woods, in an old buggy, which had seen much work, drawn by wise-looking old horses, who were reputed to have taken part in many an escapade in more youthful days. The scrub was reached where "Mrs Bruin" and her family

Going out for a bear hunt.

were in hiding, and the guns were posted on a hillside commànding a delightful view of the lake for sketching purposes, and our bear hunters, with their dogs, plunged about bravely round the outskirts of the thicket, which was too dense and prickly for anyone to penetrate, except

Guisachan Farm. 171

at the risk of clothes and skin. There was much hallooing, and barking of dogs, and beating with sticks; but no results, though every now and then a glimpse of the brown fur was caught by one or other of the sportsmen, and the end of it all was that we were obliged to own that "Mrs Bruin" was cleverer than we, for all of a

Watching the game-bag.

sudden she was spied scuttling up a hill a quarter-of-a-mile distant, having got away by a side where there was no gun posted, and having determined to leave her children in the lurch. So we had to satisfy ourselves with having seen her, and we wended our way home under a glorious sunset sky, with hundreds of wild geese flying to their feeding grounds, filling the air with their wild, peculiar cries. I will not tell you how many of them were brought down on this occasion! but I can tell

"Foo," our Chinese cook.

you wild goose is very good, and so are some of the other game birds which were provided for us by our sportsmen during our stay at Guisachan. There are the wild duck, of which there are several varieties on the Okanagan Lake, and which bring to our minds an exciting chase, and a brilliant long shot by my brother, such as sportsmen love to think back on, and good retrieving on the part of good dog "Spot." Then there are the "ruffed grouse," more like our pheasant to eat, and what is called the "prairie chicken," so named by early settlers, but which in reality

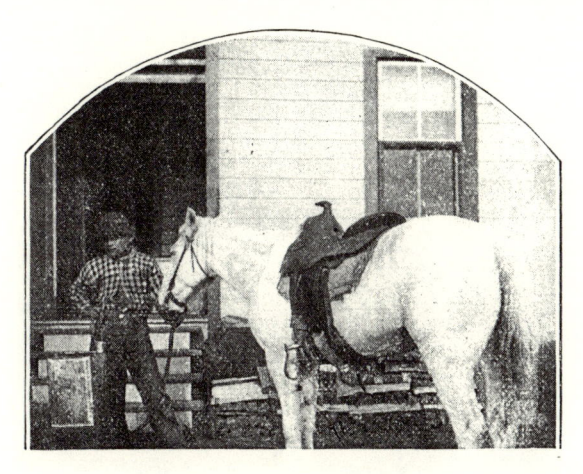

Willy, the Indian boy, with his white pony.

is a species of grouse, and, in our opinion, the best game bird for the table which Canada possesses. And bear steak and chops are very good, too; for one of those rash young bears was killed after all, and though he was very thin, poor little chap, yet we thought him a good substitute for venison, as served up by "Foo," our Chinese cook.

The mention of that dignitary reminds me that I have not yet introduced you to our establishment, nor shown you over the house. Well, first, besides ourselves, our little girl, Marjorie, my brother Coutts, and Mr Smith,

Residence No 1. Present owner emerging from inspection.

there is Barron, my maid, the companion of all our journeyings for many years past, and who knows most quarters of the globe, is a perfect traveller, is never sea sick, never has headaches, and never forgets anything. At Guisachan she became a sort of combined housekeeper and housemaid. Then comes Turner, Lord A.'s servant, another valuable companion of our wanderings, and who, on the present occasion, showed his usual energy and adaptability in every *rôle* from butler to woodchopper. "Foo," who on ordinary occasions was general factotum, accepted such assistance with alacrity, and showed his appreciation by never appearing in his kitchen till half-past eight in the morning. Did we remonstrate? Oh, no; we knew better. A Chinese cook is a very

Residence No. 2.

touchy gentleman, and if you offend his majesty you will find that he will demand his pay and walk off the next hour. And we got into terrible trouble one day. A large covey of prairie chicken flew past the house. Lord A. ran to get his gun; but, meanwhile, friend "Foo" had seen the birds, and, being fond of sport, borrowed my brother's gun and ammunition out of his room, without saying "by your leave," and sped away so as to be first on the scene of action. On being called back, and a humble suggestion made that he should wait a minute and go *with* Lord A., instead of *in front* of him, he waxed fierce with wrath, and not only did he rush ahead and scatter the birds, but for a day or two afterwards retired

Residence No. 3.

into the sulks, varied with ebullitions of wrath over the unwarrantable interference with his liberties which had occurred. But, nevertheless, he was a good cook, as most of the Chinese are, and, when all is said, it is hard to see how the British Columbian folk could get on without the Chinese servants and labourers. You see

Residence No. 4.

them everywhere, and they are ready to be combined cook, groom, housemaid, and gardener, and the general verdict is that, after all, they are better than girls who come out from the old country with all sorts of foolish notions in their heads as to what work they should or should not do. I regret to say that the general tone of the girls who have gone to British Columbia, and who get high wages (12, 15, and 20 dollars a month, and even more), has not been such as to make employers very anxious to repeat the experiment. Still, girls going West to the Pacific coast are certain to find good places, and if only they will be sensible, and ready to turn their hands to anything, and to do as they are bid, they will command first-rate wages and happy homes. In the meanwhile the Chinaman has still the predominance, and he possesses many advantages, though his wages are high. But I must come back to our Guisachan establishment, and introduce you to Willy, an Indian boy, who arrived every morning on his white pony at full gallop, and who was initiated into the mysteries of blacking boots, and the greater mystery of picking up "Foo's" tins and empty bottles, feathers, and other *débris*, so as to make the place look a bit tidy.

Now, take a peep round the house, into the hall decorated with horns and heads of deer shot in Dakota by my brother, and with various specimens of Indian work; and then see the pretty bright sitting-room, with

The Guisachan staff

skins of animals, shot in the same way, scattered about on the floor: pictures on the walls, and magazines and other evidences of the last mail on the table; the dining-room at the back, to which communication is obtained from the kitchen across a passage open to the air, thus devised with the object of avoiding unnecessary kitchen

Starting for a drive with " Charlie" and " Pinto."

smells, four big bed-rooms, two small ones, the office, and a broad verandah round three sides of the house, will complete the survey. It is the fourth mansion on the Guisachan estate, and we give you a sight of the four. The first as you see is a mere " shack," evidently put up for shelter on the owner's first arrival. The second, though in ruins now, was doubtless a good enough house for the country in its day. The third is quite a big house, with two good living rooms in it, and is now inhabited by the men. It looks quite smart, now

Mr Smith exhibiting the wild Indian pony.

that it has peen painted outside and inside, and the sundry traces of the former occupants done away with. Many tales of the wild doings of these Macdougalls were told us, and testimony to the truth of some, at least, of these was to be seen in the marks of the pistol shots with which the walls and ceiling of the house were riddled.

We were fortunate in securing a very nice set of men, and I am sorry our Kodak has not done them more justice. They were gathered from all parts of the country, and from all sorts and conditions of men—one would be from Ontario, another from Yorkshire, another from the States; another was the son of a gentleman near London, who unexpectedly arrived one evening to spend a few hours with his boy. This young man owned a farm in Alberta, but was hiring himself out as a workman in order to get the wherewithal to carry on his farm more efficiently.

The foreman, Frank Conckling, was an old friend of my brother's in Dakota, and most valuable acquisition, for he is one of those handy-men who can turn to anything and do it all well. He has now brought his father from the Eastern States to live with him. Both have a knowledge of fruit-growing, and are taking up some land of their own.

With the high wages obtained in British Columbia (45 to 50 dollars a month for a foreman, and 30 to 35 for an ordinary workman, with board and lodgings provided), a saving and sober man can soon save up enough to make a start on his own account. It is sad to hear, however, of the many ruined lives and fortunes which must be put down to the influence of strong drink and the saloon.

Guisachan Farm.

Numbers of small farms in the district which we are now

Coutts on "Aleck"—"Spot" in attendance

describing have been literally drunk away and are now the

property of the license-holders. It is to be hoped that the new settlers coming into the valley will help to promote social gatherings and entertainments, which will meet the natural desire for gathering together in a cheery way, without sowing the seeds of intemperance and misery.

Our neighbours were good enough to gather in our house twice during our stay, and thus welcomed the new-comers, and made us feel real Okanaganers. One of these gatherings was in the evening, and was just an old-fashioned Scotch "social," with tea and "bags" of eatables handed round, or rather, to be strictly accurate, we had the eatables without the bags. And a very pleasant evening we had, with songs, and music, and recitations, some in English and some in French, for the benefit of our French Roman Catholic neighbours, who represent the earlier settlers all round what is termed the "Okanagan Mission." The Mission was founded some 32 years ago for the Indians, by a devoted priest, Father Pendozy, of whose fame we heard much, and who only died a few months before our arrival. The Indians have mostly moved away to their reserve at the foot of the lake, but "the Mission" is now the head-quarters of a large district, and it is also the residence of a lay brotherhood who cultivate a farm and orchard. The two priests in residence, Father Marzial and Father de Vriendt, were both amongst our guests at our "social," and the latter gave us two songs, while the Presbyterian minister, Mr. Langell, gave us a recitation. It was the first time that such a gathering had been held in the district, but from the success which attended it, we hope it will not be the last. Since then a magic-lantern has been established at Guisachan, and we hear that the first magic-lantern entertainment was well attended and much liked.

The other gathering of which I spoke was a little Sunday afternoon service conducted by Lord A. That really came first, on our first Sunday, and was intended as a sort of formal taking possession and dedication of the house, and it was delightful to find all our neighbours, both Protestant and Roman Catholic, gathering together for the occasion. Some sort of gathering, such as this, on the Sunday afternoon or evening, has also become another institution at Guisachan.

But the mention of a service reminds me that I must tell you how active the Presbyterian Church in Canada is in providing services for colonies of new settlers. We were much struck with this throughout our trip. Even in quite small places where we halted, we found that provision was made for at least fortnightly services, and a missionary appointed, who is paid out of a Home Mission Fund, collected mainly by the zealous Dr. Robertson, until such time as the young community can afford to pay for their own church and minister. Our friend,

Mr Gordon of Banff, told us that experience justified this action. If settlers are allowed to get into a habit of not attending church, it will be generally much longer before they move in the matter themselves than when the means of grace have been placed within their reach from the beginning, and many opportunities for promoting religious influences, and for preventing evil will have been lost. In the Okanagan Valley there is a service now every Sunday; at the upper end one Sunday, at the house of some good neighbours, the Postills, and at our end the next Sunday, at the Schoolhouse, which the Board have gladly lent for the purpose, although several-of the members are Roman Catholics. At the present time the minister lives in Vernon, 35 miles away, and has to return there always in time for an evening service. But already there is more than a talk of two churches, one at either end of the valley, and a minister of our own. We shall never forget the picturesqueness of the scene which met our eye as we drove up to the Schoolhouse for the morning service. As usual the weather was gorgeous. The School is situated just at the corner of a wood of tall trees gay in their brilliant autumn colourings. Just inside this wood, and on its outskirts, were tied up saddle horses and buggies of all sizes and descriptions, and all around were standing picturesque groups of men and dogs awaiting the moment for going in. The brilliant sunshine pouring down on the scene

Planting Scotch firs from Guisachan, Inverness-shire, at Guisachan, B. C.

and glinting on the stems of the trees completed the charm and naturalness of the picture. No conventionality, no black coats, no formal solemnity. There were but three women in the congregation; all the rest were men and lads who looked as if they knew how to work. Mr Langell quite adopted the same free and easy attitude, and spoke to his hearers as if he were one of them. I am so sorry that I cannot give you a picture of that scene outside the church, and I would have liked to put in the very forefront, the dearest and cheeriest of old ladies, in an old-fashioned black poke bonnet—Mrs Postill, who had driven over 16 miles or so with her son, and who told us she had been the first white woman in the valley, and that she would never forget all the kindness shown her in those old days by the rough miners and ranchers.

But all this while I am telling you nothing about the farm itself. But where shall I begin? Shall I describe to you the cattle which we took over with the farm, and which may be found anywhere within a 20 mile radius, or the cows who did not at all understand that their mission in life was to provide milk for the human species? At the outset some of these same cows resented the idea so fiercely that they had to be lassoed and thrown on their sides to be milked. When we were there they had somewhat reconciled themselves to the new order of things, but the milkers had still to go and search for them on horseback.

Or shall I show you our stud of horses—the old team, and the new team, with the foal, Madge, who after the fashion of the country, accompanied her mother when out for work, and insisted always on running just in front and so impeding progress; the old white pack horse, and canny Aleck, and pretty Harry from Dakota, and Pinto, and wise old thirty-year-old Charlie, who was none too old, however, to give our little girl many a delightful canter, and who was a much more reliable steed than the wild Indian pony which had been intended for her use, but who absolutely refused to bear the indignity of any mortal on its back, and who made good its escape to its free companions, bridled and saddled, more than once, and had to be re-captured.

No; I do not think that I will detain you here, nor will I ask you to admire what is called the "barn" in Canada, but what we should call the stable. I may confess that that building is not in the best of repair. Nor will I ask you to admire our pigs, among which we boast of some Berkshires; nor our white Leghorns, nor even will I linger to point out the fascinating antics of the beautiful but hated blue jays, the enemies of both farmer and gardener; nor the pranks of the magpies, who often made the place lively with their chatterings and their quarrellings over some coveted bone or other choice scrap.

No, but I will ask you to take a passing look at the baby fir-trees which we brought out from the old Guisachan, in Inverness-shire, to be planted at the new Guisachan. For "Guisachan" means "The Place of the Fir," and though there are many firs all round about on the mountains, there were none quite near the house; and then I must call upon you to admire our cabbages, any one of which would require an ordinary wheelbarrow as a conveyance; and then look at our glorious melons, and citrons, and cucumbers, and apples, even as we saw them so late as in October. Unfortunately our photographs turned out failures, so you must take our word for it when we tell you that the melons often weigh 30 lbs. and more; and also when we give you the following example of what an ordinary orchard produces in this country. Our next door neighbour has an orchard of about a third of an acre containing twenty-four apple trees, half of which are old trees and the others young, some as young as four years old. This gentleman and his wife have a family of four little boys, and take in lodgers besides, having sometimes in the summer as many as fourteen boarders. The produce of the orchard forms a never-failing item in the menu, and one of the lodgers told us he could never have believed that apples could be cooked in so many different excellent ways till he went to lodge with Mrs Monson. But after the powers of the orchard had been thus taxed all through

Guisachan Farm.   191

the fruit season, the owner was able to sell the residue of the produce for 250 dollars. And such apples! Such facts, and the knowledge of the ever-increasing demand for fruit of all kinds in the North-West Provinces, will

S.S. "Penticton" waiting to bear us away.

doubtless cause the valley to become ere long a great fruit-producing centre. Two hundred acres of the Guisachan farm will be planted with various kinds of fruit-trees this year, and with the smaller kinds of fruit, such as strawberries, raspberries, blackberries, currants, and gooseberries in between. All these fruits, as well as the apples, pears, plums, melons, &c., flourish magnificently and with the best possible results. Peaches and grapes have also been tried, but we did not ourselves think the specimens we saw were satisfactory. A number of purchasers have been taking up the lots subdivided for fruit farms by Mr G. G. Mackay, who set a good example in the neighbourhood by buying estates and dividing them into lots. Hops, wheat, barley, and all root crops yield abundantly, the wheat averaging 35 bushels an acre. Good land for fruit growing is now fetching from 30 to 60 dollars an acre, and is steadily rising in value. A land owner in the neighbourhood, owning a ranch which consists of some 4000 to 5000 acres of rough hill range land, and 500 acres of good rich agricultural land, was offered 36,000 dollars for the whole. "Not I," says he, "Not a farthing less will I take than 90,000 dollars for the property." "Then do you think the men fools who are selling their land for 60 dollars an acre?" That is just what I do think them. I know the worth of that land, I tell you." The steady rise in price, which is going on so far, justifies this opinion. There was one difficulty in the way of the grower of small and perishable fruits, and that was the difficulty about their transit, for though the demand for fresh fruit is great, it of course cannot be carried any great distance without injury. This has now been obviated by Lord Aberdeen deciding to put up a jam factory and cannery, at the head of the lake near Vernon, where all good fruit raised in the district can be received, and this announcement has been greeted with

Good-bye!

great satisfaction. The site of the factory has been placed near Vernon, both on account of the proximity to the railway, and because it is near the Coldstream property, which now belongs to Lord A., and part of which he has entrusted to Mr Mackay [1] for subdivision into the fruit farms which appear to be so much wanted, or fruit farms combined with grazing ground, for those who wish to raise cattle or keep dairy stock, for which there are good openings.

We are often asked for advice as to what class of settlers are likely to succeed in this part of British Columbia. There are two classes whom the country will suit. (1) Men with a little capital, say not less than £500, who can buy 20 acres perhaps or more, have the means to plant it and cultivate it, put up a little frame house and be able to support themselves until the fruit begins to bear. It takes four or five years for apple trees to bear, but of course many of the other kinds of crops and fruits bear the second or even the first year. A fruit-grower who is keen about his trees will have each tree numbered and entered in a book, and will find delightful occupation in carefully nurturing, pruning, and watching over each young nursling, while he may expect an abundant reward by-and-bye. There are some College graduates now taking up land in our district, some of whom came thinking of following the learned professions, but finding these all full, are very sensibly devoting themselves to

[1] Since the above was written, we grieve to say that Mr G. G. Mackay died suddenly (in January 1893), much regretted by his friends and neighbours.

fruit-farming. (2) The second class of men who can succeed are those who will hire themselves out as labourers, and who will set themselves to save their high wages and meanwhile learn the ways of the country.

We are hopeful that a very good class of settler is coming in amongst us, which will make the district a desirable one for those who seek to find a home where there will be good influences and a high tone.

I must not forget to mention that the climate and its healthfulness are great attractions. We certainly found the climate a most perfect and health-giving one during our all too brief sojourn; but my brother gave it the same character, as also did the old residents of the valley, who seem never to have found out the need for a doctor. The weather was a perfect "Indian summer," while we were there at the end of October. They have, we understand, about six weeks' hard winter with thermometer often considerably below zero, and two months of the summer are very hot, and the mosquitoes abound far more than *we* should like. But, taking it all round, the people seem wholly satisfied with their weather. Certain it is that we at least agree with Mr Mackay when he said, in a letter to the papers, that "if a man cannot be happy here he can be happy nowhere,"—nor a woman either, say I.

Now Lord A. says I have been writing a puff, and let my enthusiasm for our holiday-resort run away with **me**, but he has to admit that all that I have said is true—and he often wishes he were there.

I am afraid I have occupied an altogether unwarrantable amount of space in the Magazine this month, and even now, I shall not be able to include the pictures of the Coldstream Ranch in this month's issue. We felt very badly when we had to wend our way to the point of embarkation, and sadly say good-bye and sail up the Lake to Vernon, under charge of good Captain Shorts, who knows the country well, and who fell in with our humour by singing its praises.

XIII.

THE INDIANS OF CANADA.

YOU saw us off from Guisachan a few weeks ago, and now this month I am afraid we must bid Good-bye to British Columbia, though I would gladly linger there with you awhile, and chatter on about our further experiences whilst in that charming province, and about all our plans for the future. But it will be better to wait awhile until I can tell you whether our customers at Vernon are satisfied with our dairy supplies from the Coldstream, and until I can explain to you the process by which we mean to try to turn out the best jams and preserves in the Dominion. When you get a chance of buying "Oka jam," mind you seize it, for nothing will equal it, I am sure!!

Before we leave the subject, however, I must tell you about the Coldstream Ranch, which is the name of the large property which Lord Aberdeen has bought near Vernon.

Not such a smart house as at Guisachan, but there is a good barn standing by the side of the house, and in the other pictures you will see some specimens of our Coldstream horses and cattle, though some of the creatures have spoiled their likenesses by moving whilst being photographed. You cannot judge from these pictures of the beauty of the valley, which received the following description from a business gentleman who was sent lately to survey it:—" I wish you had been with me, and I think you would agree that it is not only one of the richest but one of the most beautiful valleys you ever saw." It receives its name from a stream which is always ice-cold even in our hottest weather. A considerable portion of the property runs along the shores of the lovely "Long Lake," pronounced by Lord Lorne to be one of the most attractive sheets of water he had seen in America. We had a good view of the lake from a spot where we picnicked one day during an expedition from Guisachan. This was at the other end of the lake from that on which the Coldstream is situated, and where residences are being erected on the shores, on "lots" which have already been parcelled off from the property. There is a curious feature about this lake: One can see stretching across the lake what looks like a bridge or dam. It goes in the district by the name of "the Railway," and is in reality the work of the skilful beaver architects and workers.

And now will you travel down with us to the coast, and see the "Empress of India" start from Vancouver

Going to work at Coldstream Ranch.

bound for Japan, China, and India? She is one of the three grand new ships built by the Canadian Pacific Railway, which now make communication between China, Japan, Canada, and England so easy and swift, that it is possible for letters from Japan to reach London in twenty days.

We were very glad to have a chance of seeing over the comfortable internal arrangements of the ship, with a view of a possible expedition in the future to that wonderful country, to pick up gossip for you; and even our aversion to the sea did not prevent us from half-envying our friends when we saw them making their start, amidst the cheers of the Vancouver public, who take vast interest in these boats, which are so greatly promoting the prosperity of their city and province. Amongst the living freight carried on this occasion was a crowd of Chinamen on the lower deck, who, having made their fortunes, were returning home to their own land. It creates a curious sensation to be brought face to face with this strange people between whom and ourselves there seems to be a gulf fixed—the two races having so little in common, and yet, at anyrate in British Columbia, depending so largely on one another. They despise us, and look on us as heathens, and are unwilling to let their dead bodies be contaminated by resting in our soil, but endeavour to have them all back to China for interment. And we, or at least many of us, no less unjustly despise them, and

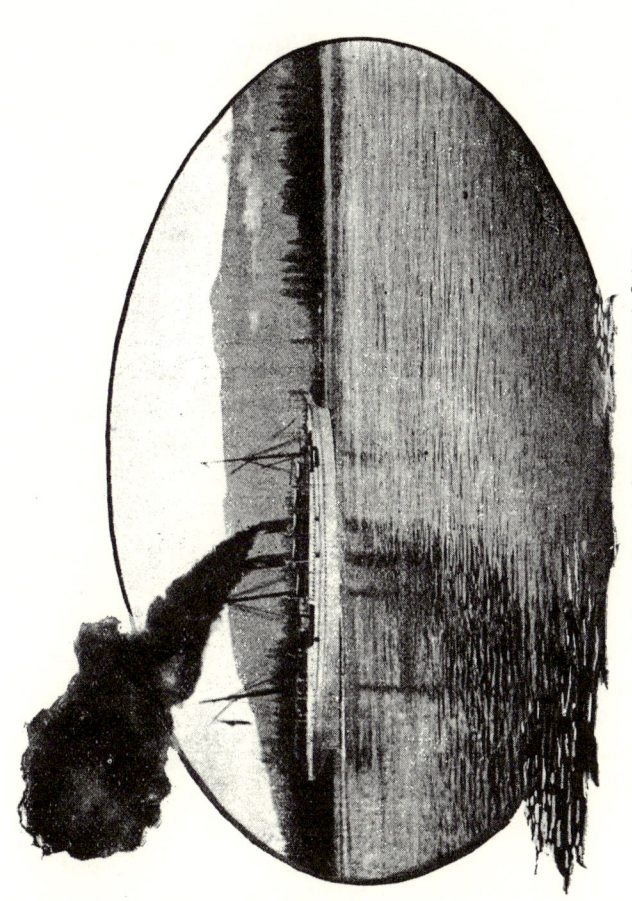

The s.s. "Empress of India" steaming out of Vancouver, en route to Japan.

call them "Heathen Chinee," having but scant respect for the great forces lying hidden in that vast "Celestial Empire," of whose internal affairs and workings we are comparatively so ignorant.

But it was not of the Chinese that I was to talk in this paper, but of another race with whom we are far more immediately concerned, and concerning whom we have far more responsibility. As you pass through Canada from east to west, through her thick forests and over her wide prairies, and her mighty mountains, it is a pathetic sight to see what appear to be the ghosts of a people of other days, stealing, gaunt and mournful, and silent, to the towns and railway stations, and who, crouching around, watch the new race rising up and possessing this fair and goodly land over which *they* held sovereign sway in the times now gone by. They are an unattractive sight, with their deeply-lined countenances, and prominent features, bedaubed often with paint, their black dishevelled hair, their array of ragged squalid blankets, or tattered garments, to which fragments of tawdry finery give the finishing touch to an aspect of distasteful wretchedness. Perchance, mingling with a reflection of national self-complacency that the Canadian Government have on the whole dealt fairly and justly with these Indians within her borders, there comes also a scarcely acknowledged thought that it is as well for these poor folk that their race is yearly diminishing, and that by-and-bye all traces of their existence will have vanished, save in museums.

But can we thus lightly dismiss the fate and fortunes of a nation whom we have disinherited? Think of their position a few years ago, ere the buffalo disappeared before the advance of the white man. They were wealthy in those days, wealthy after the only fashion about which they cared aught. The vast plains were their undisputed hunting-ground, and the unnumbered herds of buffaloes provided for all their needs. *Food*, for they lived chiefly on buffalo, eating sometimes as much as eight or ten lbs. a day; *houses*, for the tanned skins made comfortable and durable tents, or "tee-pees," or "lodges" as they call them; *clothing*, for from them they obtained their robes and other articles of clothing. They had bands of horses and ponies to transport them and their goods to a fresh location, whensoever it pleased them to move, and to carry them to the chase of the wild beasts and birds, in which they so excelled. What more did they need?

Now they are confined to certain portions of the country alloted to them by Government, called "Indian reserves"; they are poor, for the buffalo has mysteriously disappeared within the last twelve or fifteen years, and they have to depend in large measure on the charity of Government, which gives them rations of food to save them from starvation; the wild animals and birds which they loved to pursue, which supplied them with food and ornaments, and for which they commanded a ready sale, are fast diminishing; they are suffering from diseases and vices introduced by the "pale-faces"; and their ideas of life and civilisation so totally differ from those of their conquerors that it is with the utmost difficulty they can set themselves to win their livelihood by what appears to them the dull and distasteful work of agriculture. Small wonder that the red man looks sad, and listless, and hopeless, as he looks out on the altered conditions of life for his race, and as he meditates on the future of his country, which seems to have so little place for him unless he alters all his habits and tastes! An earnest effort is being made, both by missionaries and by the Government, to help him to accommodate himself to the new conditions, but it is uphill work. But there is often an instinctive want of trust between the two races, and a lack of understanding of one another. Wise men of science, and sympathetic and large-minded missionaries, are both now searching into the customs, habits, and traditions of the different tribes of North American Indians, and with a wider knowledge of these there will come fuller power to enter into their ideas and conceptions, to gain their confidence, and consequently their co-operation in the work of their own elevation and civilisation.

Our ideas of the Red Indian are largely the outcome of the representation of him in the stirring tales of daring adventure and cruel ferocity, which are considered the fittest literature for boys—but we go no further.

I would like to interest you in another way in these children of the plain and forest, but my knowledge is so fragmentary and inadequate that I can only give you glimpses into that little understood world of the Indian. As you know, there are many different tribes, from those of the East, who received the white men so hospitably on their first appearance, but who afterwards became so dreaded, to those in the extreme West in British Columbia, who appear to be so distinct in character and customs from those east of the Rocky Mountains that I will defer all mention of them until another paper. Amongst all these different tribes the chief religion appears to consist in a belief of spirits, spirits which inhabit earth, air, water, as also animals, and even inanimate things, and whose protection must be sought, and whose vengeance avoided. They do not, however, like other heathen people, make images or idols of these spirits, and their chief reverence is given to the sun and moon, and to one Chief Spirit, who re-appears in the legends of various tribes under different names, and in many characters.

Let me give you here one or two examples of their religious traditions, as taken down from their own lips by the Rev. E. Wilson, and reported by him to the British Association:—

THE CREATION.—"It had been long time night. Napi, the Ancient, said, 'Let it be day,' and it became day. Napi made the sun, and told it to travel from east to west. Every night it sinks into the earth, and it comes out of the earth again the next morning. Napi is very old every winter, but he becomes young every spring. He has travelled all along the Rocky Mountains, and there are various marks on the mountains which remain as relics of his presence. Napi said, 'We will be two people.' He took out the lower rib from his right side, and he said, 'It shall be a woman,' and he let it go, and he looked on it, and he saw a woman. He then took a rib from the left side, and said, 'Let it be a boy,' and it was a boy. Napi also made a number of men with earth. Napi and the men went one way, the woman went another way. And the woman made women of earth, in the same way as Napi had made men.

"At Morley, opposite the Rev. Mr Macdougall's house, and down the river," said Big Plume, "there is a little stream; they call it the men's kraal or enclosure; on one side of the stream is a cut bank and big stones; this was the men's boundary, beyond which they were not to pass. They used to hunt buffalo, and drive them over the cut bank; they had plenty of meat; they had no need to follow the buffaloes; they hid themselves behind the big stones and uttered a low cry; this guided the buffalo to the cut bank, and when they were over the bank they shot them with their stone arrows and ate the meat.

"One day Napi went out on a long journey. He got as far as High River. There he saw lots of women together, with the woman made from his rib, who acted as their chief. There were no men and no boys there. There were a great number of teepees. Napi was alone. He told the women, 'I have come from the men.' The woman chief said to him, 'Go home; bring all your men; stand them all on the top of this stone ridge; our women shall then go up one by one, and each take a man for a husband.' When they were all up there, the chief woman went up first and laid hold on Napi to take him, but Napi drew back; the chief woman had put on an old and torn blanket, and had rubbed all the paint off her face, and had no ornaments on her. Napi did not like her appearance, and so he rejected her addresses. He did not know that she was the chief woman. She then went back to the women, and, pointing to Napi, said, 'Don't any of you take him.' She then dressed herself in her best, and painted her face, and put on her ornaments, and went and chose another man. All the women did the same. Thus all the men had wives, and Napi was left standing alone. The chief woman then cried aloud, 'Let him stand there alone like a pine tree.' Napi then began breaking away the stony ridge with his heel, till there was only very little of it left. The woman then shouted, 'Be a pine tree.' And the pine tree stands there now alongside the big stones, and they still call it the women's kraal. Napi's flesh is in the pine tree, but his spirit still wanders through the earth.

"The boy made from Napi's left rib fell sick. The woman took a stone and threw it in the water, and she said, 'If the stone swims the boy will live,' but the stone sank and the boy died; and so all people die now. If the stone had floated, all people would have lived."

HOW HORSES ORIGINATED.—"A long time ago there were no horses. There were only dogs. They used only stone for their arrows. They were fighting with people in the Rocky Mountains. Those people were Snake Indians. They took a Blackfoot woman away south. There were a great number of people down there, and they tied the woman's feet, and tied her hands behind her, and a cord round her waist, and picketed her to a stake, near the big salt water. And they cried across the lake, 'See, here is your wife!' Then they all retreated and left her. These Big Lake people did not see her at all; but the waters rose and covered her; and when the waters abated, there was no woman there, but there were lots of horses. The Snake Indians caught these horses, and that is how horses began."

FUTURE LIFE.—"I asked 'Big Plume' what did he think became of the soul after death? He replied that the souls of all Blackfeet Indians go to the Sandhills, north of the Cyprus hills (this would be to the east of the Blackfeet country). What proof had he of that? I asked. 'At a distance,' said the chief, 'we can see them hunting buffalo, and we can hear them talking and praying, and inviting one another to their feasts. In the summer we often go there, and we see the trails of the spirits, and the places where they have been camping. I have been there myself, and have seen them, and heard them beating their drums. We can see them in the distance, but when we get near to them they vanish. I cannot say whether or not they see the Great Spirit. I believe they will live for ever. All the Blackfeet believe this; also the Sarcees, Stonies, Atsinas, and Crees. The Crees, after death, will go to the Sandhills further north. There will still be fighting between the Crees and the Blackfeet in the spiritual world. Dogs and horses go to the Sandhills too; also the spirits of the dead buffaloes. We hand these traditions down to our children. We point out to our children various places where Napi slept, or walked, or hunted, and thus our children's minds become impressed.'"

You have probably heard of the Indians' *medicine-bags*, and the name suggests that medicines are carried about for cases of emergency, but their ideas of medicine and ours are two very different affairs. When a young man grows up he has to find out which of the many spirits is to be his special protector, and then he has to carry the symbol of this spirit always on his person as a sort of charm.

(From a photograph by Boorne & May.)

And here is an account, by Mr Hale, of the way they find their "medicine":—

"Young men go up on to a hill and cry and pray for some animal or bird to come to them. Before starting out they wash themselves all over, and put off all their clothing and ornaments, except a blanket. For five or six days they neither eat nor drink, and they become thin. They take a pipe with them, and tinder and flint, and a native weed or bark for smoking (not matches or tobacco). When the pipe is filled they point the stem to the sun, and say, 'Pity me, that some animal or bird may come to me!' Then they address the trees, the grass, the water, and the stones in the same manner If any one crosses their path while so engaged, they call aloud to them to warn them off, saying, 'I am living alone; do not come near!' While in this state they dream, and whatever animal or bird they see in their dream becomes their medicine or guardian through life. They are told also in a dream what description of herbs or roots to gather as their medicine, and this they collect and put carefully into a small bag to keep as a charm. They also kill the animal they dreamed of, and keep its skin as a charm. No one knows what is the medicine they have gathered; it is kept a profound secret. The little bag is kept in the tent, and no one may touch it but the owner, other Indians would be afraid to meddle with it. There is no particular age for young men to engage in the above rites. They start away in the evening—only in summer. Some go of their own accord, others are bid to do so by their fathers or elder brothers. If they do not go, any sickness that comes upon them will certainly be fatal, or if shot by an enemy they will certainly die."

The burial customs bring out again the same belief in spirits, inasmuch as they bury the dead person's belongings with him, and kill his pony, so that the spirits of these things may be at hand for his use in the other world.

"The Blackfeet never bury their dead below the surface of the soil; they think it a horrible practice to expose the body to the worms and vermin that live in the ground. They either deposit the bodies on a hill-top or place them in a tree. Perhaps, being sun-worshippers, their idea is that the sun should still shine upon them after they are dead. When the body is placed in a tree it is wrapped in blankets and put up on a rudely-constructed platform. When deposited on a hill-top, or cliff, a rough kind of box is made, three times the size of a coffin, and into it are put, besides the body, all that belonged to the dead person—blankets, saddle, gun, kettles, and everything; it is then nailed down, dragged by a pony on a *travoie* to the appointed spot, and there deposited. Sometimes a few logs are piled round it to keep off the dogs and wild animals, but often nothing is to be seen but the rudely-made box and some kind of flag flying above it. When a chief dies his favourite pony is brought and killed at the door of his tent; his body is then laid out in his own teepee, often in a sitting position, and all his possessions are spread around him; the edges of the tent are wedged down and secured with stones, then the teepee is closed and left. This is called a 'death teepee.' Travellers sometimes come across a solitary teepee, with no signs of life around it, and, on looking in, are horrified to see a decomposing corpse. There is great grief when a person dies. The people weep and howl over the dead bodies of their friends. It is usual also for the friends to throw their blankets and other valuables into the coffin before it is closed. A mother has been known to wrap her last remaining blanket around her dead infant, even in the middle of winter. Mr Tims told me of a father walking several miles barefooted through the snow to bury his little child, having given his moccasins to his dead infant. The graves of the dead are visited by the living; the people often come and hold a feast with the departed spirits, setting aside portions of food for them. The Blackfeet seem to have no dread of ghosts or spirits, and do not mind handling dead bodies. It is not an unusual thing for a 'death teepee' even to be rifled by those bent on plunder."

XIV.

MORE ABOUT THE INDIANS AND THEIR CUSTOMS.

NOW let me show you a picture of the fine old Indian Chief, "Crowfoot," whose physiognomy and expression will tell you of the strength of character and mind that lay behind. He was one of the far-seeing Indians who understood that it was for the ultimate good of the country that the white men should take possession of the country, that railways should traverse its length and breadth, though bringing destruction to the Red Men's hunting-grounds, and that the land should be brought under the dominion of the plough. He saw that the only hope for the Indian was to accommodate himself to the new order of things, and to co-operate with the Englishmen in spreading education, and civilisation, and the art of agriculture. He was of great service to the Government when the great railway across the Continent was planned, and in many other ways managed to bring his people to help, and not to hinder. In recognition of these services he was given a pass (which you see him wearing in the picture) not only over the C.P.R., but

"Crowfoot," Chief of the Blackfeet.

214   Through Canada with a Kodak.

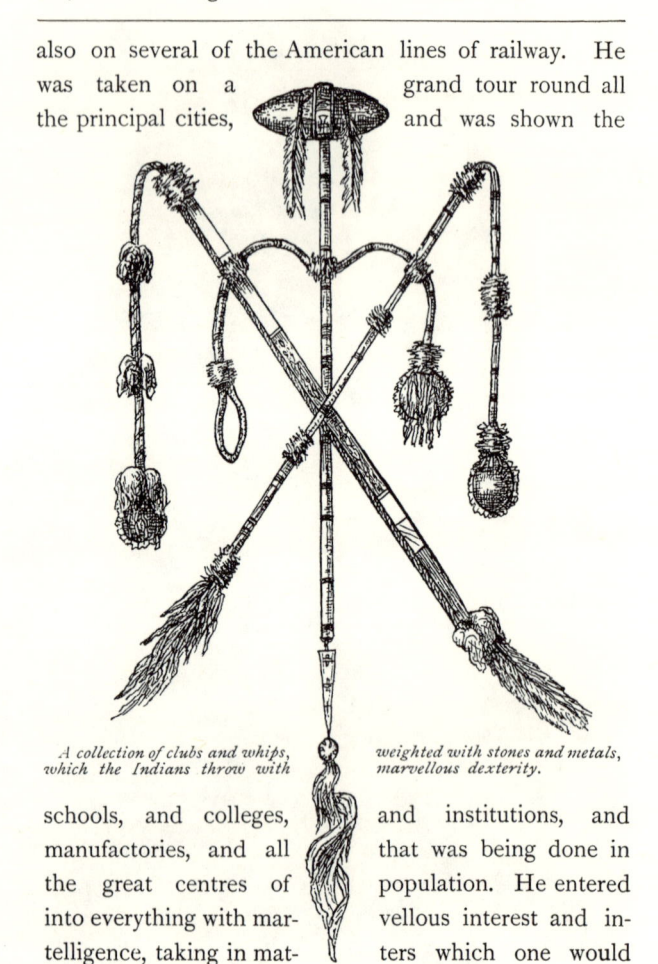

also on several of the American lines of railway. He was taken on a grand tour round all the principal cities, and was shown the

A collection of clubs and whips, which the Indians throw with weighted with stones and metals, marvellous dexterity.

schools, and colleges, and institutions, and manufactories, and all that was being done in the great centres of population. He entered into everything with mar- vellous interest and in- telligence, taking in mat- ters which one would have thought totally beyond the comprehension of a man who had lived his life on the prairie. And when he came back to his quarters near Calgary, he gathered together his tribe, and is said to have addressed them continuously for three days, describing all the marvels that he had seen, picturing the progress of the world in terms of glowing eloquence, and how the Indians, too, might take their share in the general prosperity if they were wise in time, and would learn all that was good from the white men, without following their vices.

But Crowfoot, who died a few years back, was by no means a solitary instance of this power of oratory. Travellers and missionaries tell us that the art of swaying audiences by public speaking is very often met with, and that the speeches of the Indian orators are full of pathos and figurative beauty when heard by those who understand the language sufficiently to appreciate the force of the expressions used. Mr John Maclean, who has laboured for many years

A feather head-dress for ceremonial and war dances. It is worn down the back of the head.

amongst the Indians in Alberta, gives us various illustrations of such speeches in his interesting book on "The Indians and their Manners and Customs." We may take as an example part of a speech by "Tecumseh," who, at the beginning of this century, helped the British so heroically in the war against the Americans. When General Brock, in command of the British troops, was preparing to retreat into Canada, on hearing of the defeat of our fleet on Lake Erie, he concealed the news of the defeat from Tecumseh, fearing that it would have a bad effect on his Indian allies. Tecumseh, who had but a poor opinion of Brock, addressed him thus at a Council :—

> "Father, listen! Our fleet has gone out; we know they have fought; we have heard

belt of feathers worn in time of war and at ceremonial dances.

the great guns; but we know nothing of what has happened to our father with the one arm (Captain Barclay). Our ships have gone one way, and we are much astonished to see our father tying up everything, and preparing to run the other way, without letting his red children know what his intentions are. You always told us you would never draw your foot off British ground; but now, father, we see you drawing back, and we are sorry to see our father do so without seeing the enemy. We must compare our father's conduct to a fat dog that carries its tail upon its back, but when affrighted it drops it between its legs and runs off. Father, listen! The Americans have not defeated us by land, neither are we sure that they have done so by water; we, therefore, wish to remain here and fight our enemy, should he make his appearance. If they defeat us, then we will retreat with our father. . . . You have got the arms and ammunition which our great father, the king, sent for his red children. If you have any idea of going away, give them

A "Papoose" swathed on its cradle-board. The wooden protection at the top is arranged so that a cloth may be thrown over and protect the child from the sun. A band passes round the mother's shoulders in front. This particular cradle-board belonged to a chief's squaw, and is richly ornamented with bead work.

to us, and you may go, and welcome, for us. Our lives are in the hands of the Great Spirit. We are determined to defend our lands, and, if it be His will, we wish to leave our bones upon them."

Soon after this occasion Tecumseh was killed in battle, and his warriors took away his body and buried it in a place which no white man might ever know.

There is another feature in the character of the Indians to which we must draw special attention, and that is their wonderful and heroic endurance of pain, whether in times of war or in going through certain ceremonies required of them by their religious beliefs. Take, for instance, the sun-dance, a great ceremony amongst many of the tribes, on the occasion of which the young men are made "braves," or recognised warriors. And we must remember that the dances of the Indians, grotesque and strange as they may appear, are as sacred to them as many of our religious ceremonies. One gentleman told us that, after seeing some of his Indian friends, dressed and daubed in feathers and barbaric colours, going through all sorts of fantastic antics, to the sound of unearthly music of tom-toms and whistles and trumpets, in the streets of the town, he remonstrated with them, and asked them how such wise men as they could make such fools of themselves. And, on hearing these remonstrances, they looked much shocked and said, "But are you an unbeliever? Do you not know that this

Making a "brave" at the sun-dance. (Boorne & May).

dance is a solemn thing, a tribute that we *must* yield at this time of year to the Great Spirit." I think these words will make us recall to mind professing Christians who have much in common with these Indians whom they would look on as mere savages.

But to return to the sun-dance. On passing through an Indian reserve, near Calgary, we saw a large number of trunks of trees leaning against one central pole, forming a circle, and surmounted with what appeared a collection of rubbish, sticks, and feathers, and such like. Our guide explained to us that this is where the sun-dance takes place, though last year, owing to the persuasions of the missionaries, the ceremony did not take place, and the authorities are anxious to do all in their power to prevent its recurrence with its attendant cruel practices. We give you a picture of what a young man who desires to be made a "brave" has to go through. He first goes up to the pole in the centre, and, clasping his arms around it, prays for strength to go through the ordeal, for which he is afterwards prepared. This preparation consists in first painting the whole body a dead white, and then making a slit below two muscles in the chest, underneath which a wedge of wood is introduced. The wedge is then attached by cords to the top of the pole, and the candidate for the honours of a brave has to sway himself backwards and forwards and jerk himself until the wedge is torn out of his flesh by force. He must not utter a

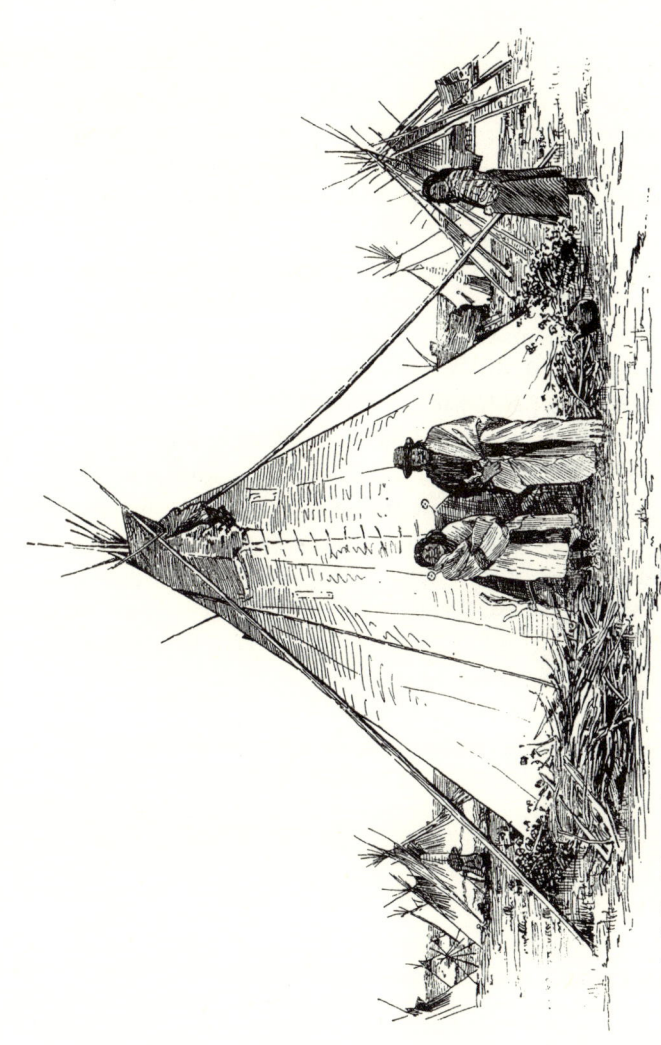

An Indian lodge or wigwam. (From a photograph by Boorne & May).

groan or a cry during the process, but is given a whistle wherewith he may divert himself, and *he* is considered the bravest who laughs and jokes most during his agony, which often lasts for hours. When the ghastly object is at last accomplished, the newly-made brave is taken charge of, often in a fainting condition, by the medicine-men, who have various processes of their own whereby to heal the cruel wounds. The bravery which is required to go through such tortures clearly shows what backbone there is in the Indian character, if it can only be made use of for the service of the God of love, and the betterment of their race, instead of for such purposes as the deliberate maiming and wounding of themselves in order to please the imaginary requirements of their Great Spirit. Many other stories could be told of the prairie tribes, which would excite our sympathy; but we must pass on in our next paper to the coast Indians, and their customs and arts, and home manufactures.

XV.

MANNERS AND TRADITIONS OF THE INDIANS OF THE COAST AND ISLANDS.

WHEN we were in Vancouver last year we had the opportunity of gathering together a small collection of Indian curios from Mr Landsberg, of Victoria, who has made a practice of collecting them for many years, and who intended having a great show of them at the Chicago "World's Fair." He gave us many interesting details regarding the use of the articles, which are now displayed on the walls of one of the corridors at Haddo House—and some of which are now reproduced for your benefit from drawings made by Mr J. Grant. But besides the information there obtained, I have also to thank the authorities of the Smithsonian Institute at Washington, where a wonderful collection of Indian curiosities is to be seen, for their readiness to allow me to make use of both printed matter and illustrations to be found in a valuable publication of theirs, written by Lieutenant Niblack, on the Coast Indians. These are my authorities; and now, what shall I pick out from these stores, to hand on to you?

You must remember, to begin with, that the Indians

Eastern part of Kasa-an Village, Prince of Wales Island, Alaska. (From "The Coast Indians of Alaska and British Columbia," by Niblack.)

of British Columbia, and especially those living on the

Manners and Traditions of Indians. 225

coast regions, on the adjacent islands and to the north in the territory of Alaska, are altogether different in manners and customs to those races of the interior about whom I have tried to tell you a little in previous papers. Their outward appearance is different too—they are of shorter height, the cheek-bones are less prominent, the nose is straighter, and the face rounder and fuller, and many hold them to be of Mongolian origin, and that they must have crossed over from Asia by the Behring Straits in times gone by. Certain it is that they had attained no small measure of civilisation and a very complex tribal organisation before the white men arrived. I will not trouble you with the names of the different tribes, nor as to which of them the special customs to which I shall refer belong; some are common to all, and some are the special property of the Salish, or the Flingit, or the Haida, as the case may be.

Now, first I will ask you to look at the picture of part of an Indian

Model of totem column erected outside an Indian house.

P

village in the Prince of Wales's Island (page 224). What do you think the carved columns in front of each house represent? "Idols," of course you will say. Nothing of the sort. These columns are carved in devices which are to them what crests are to us, and signify that the persons using that device belong to the same clan, or as they call it, the same "totem." The principal totems are the Crow, the Raven, the Bear, the Beaver, the Eagle, the Wolf, and the Whale. Representations of these animals, or of other objects which are used as the signs of totem, are carved on these totem columns outside the house, on mortuary and commemorative columns, on the articles for household and ceremonial use, and are tatooed on the skins. Look at the model of one of these columns which we have in our collection. At the top is *Hoots*, the brown bear, who is the totem of the head of the household who erected it. *Hoots* is wearing one of the grass hats, made by Indians, but the significance of this here is unknown.

Chief's ceremonial head-dress. Explained on p. 237.

Manners and Traditions of Indians. 227

Tsing, the beaver, the totem of the wife and children, is at the bottom of the column, and between the two is represented *Tetl* or *Yetl*, the great Raven, the benefactor of mankind, about whom many wonderful stories are related. His coat of feathers could be put off or on at

Mask used for ceremonial purposes and formerly for war. The Jaws move by pulling a string. The face is painted with totemic designs.

pleasure, and he had the power of transforming himself into any form he choose to assume. He existed before his birth, will never grow old and cannot die; and endless are the adventures told of his peopling the world, and providing men with fire, fresh water, fish, game, &c.,

and how he fought for them against their great enemy, *Setim-ki-jash.* Often some of these stories are illustrated on these columns, and thus they become representations, not only of the totemic relations of the household, but also of the general legends or folk-lore believed in by the tribe. But they are in no sense idols, though they represent objects which the Indian regards with superstitious respect; he believes that there exists between him and his totem an intimate and altogether special relation, which he must respect if he is to receive protection. If his totem is an animal, then he will not kill any of its class, and if it be a plant he will not cut it or gather it. Those belonging to the same totem may not marry, and thus it comes about that the wife and her children belong to a different totem to that of the head of the household. In the northern coast tribes, too, rank and wealth and property descend through the mother, according to the system known as "matriarchy" or "mother-rule," a system which has often been found to exist amongst primitive races; but in southern tribes of British Columbia this has given place to "father-rule," or

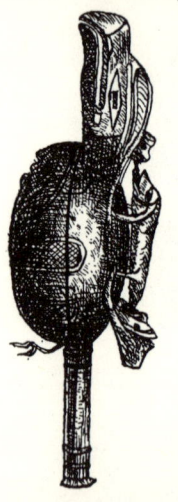

Rattle used in ceremonial dances, and also by the Shaman or medicine-man. Carved with totemic designs.

position and inheritance being obtained through the father. But if a father has special reasons for wishing his child to belong to his own totem, as, for instance, if he is a chief, and desires his son to succeed him, he must transfer him to his own totem by handing him over to his

Medicine-man's apron. Totem of eagle worked in red cloth, and below three rows of puffin beaks to rattle as wearer moves.

own sister, who will figuratively adopt him and thus change his totem.

The ties which bind the members of the same *totem* or *phratry* (an organisation in which several totems unite together in some tribes) remind us much of the ties existing between the members of our old Scottish clans. If an Indian arrives at a strange village, where he has reason to fear hostility, he will at once look out for the house whose carved post indicates that its master belongs to his totem. And *there* he is sure in any case to receive protection and to be received with honour. If, again, a member of a tribe is captured and carried off by another tribe, it is the duty of those of his own totem in the enemy's tribe to offer to redeem him and to send him back to his own tribe, when his own relatives are expected to pay back the redeemer whatever he may have expended.

The relationships and customs which spring out of these totemic organisations are endless, and full of interest, and are now receiving the investigation from men of science that they deserve. It is well that these investigations should have been set on foot, for the old ways and customs and traditions are fast disappearing, and it is only the older Indians who can give reliable information on the subject, and they are often very reticent and unwilling to give up their knowledge to strangers.

Then, again, the occasions on which the ceremonial dances and feasts, or "pot-latches," can be witnessed are becoming few and far between, owing to the discouragement given to them by the Government, who are anxious to prevent the Indians from ruining themselves and squandering their substance at these feasts, as they were wont to do. We had an opportunity, however, of seeing a whole village start forth to one of these "pot-latches," and a curious sight it was. The whole population came

Chief's coat, made of beautifully-tanned buckskin and edged with velvet and fur. These coats are often covered over with totemic designs.

forth, arrayed in garments of very diverse and very brilliant colours, and mounted their herd of scraggy little ponies. Lord Aberdeen joined a group, and tried to glean some information as to what it all meant, from an old man who was evidently of some importance amongst his fellows. But he was not communicative, and we could not at all understand why so many riderless and burdenless ponies were being driven along by the feast-goers, until it was explained to us that the important feature of a "pot-latch" was a distribution of presents to all the guests, and that these ponies were being taken so as to bear back the expected gifts. These feasts are great events in the history of a community, and are prepared for by the giver long in advance, for these are the occasions whereby men are able to advance themselves in the estimation of their fellows, and whereby they hope to attain position and honour, and possibly a chieftaincy. They are given on various occasions: on marriage, on the naming of a child, on the building of a house, or on the important occasion of the rearing of one of the carved columns previously described, and in which work the guests are all expected to assist,—or it may be given for no particular reason beyond the desire of making a figure. An ordinary man confines his invitations to the inhabit-

Fringed leggings to wear with chief's coat. Each legging used separately.

ants of his own village, but a chief invites those of the neighbouring villages also. All sorts of property are given away at a "pot-latch"—ponies, guns, canoes, robes, blankets, furs, dishes, spoons, bowls, ammunition, ornaments, and, in former times, slaves; and, according to a custom not unknown in civilised regions, the wealthy guests re-

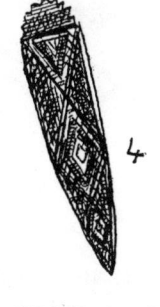

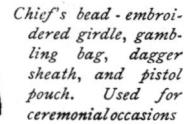

Chief's bead-embroidered girdle, gambling bag, dagger sheath, and pistol pouch. Used for ceremonial occasions

ceive the best presents, and the poor ones the shabby ones, such as a worn-out blanket or a strip of cloth. Previous to the ceremony the host gathers together his near relations, and, with their aid, makes out a list of the presents to be given to each individual. On the

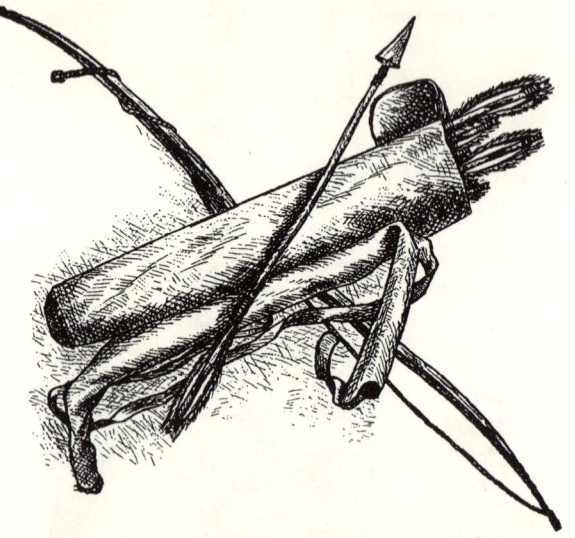

Bow and arrows and buckskin actually used by an old chief.

guests assembling, the goods are all displayed about the walls or on poles, or piled up on the floor. The host stands or sits in ceremonial attire, and presides over the affairs with a ceremonial baton in hand. The herald blows a whistle, extols the position and the virtues of the giver of the feast, calls out a name and the present which that person is to receive. The host nods his head solemnly, thumps on the floor with his baton, and an attendant takes the article and deposits it before the recipient. During the intervals, or at the end, dancing, feasting,

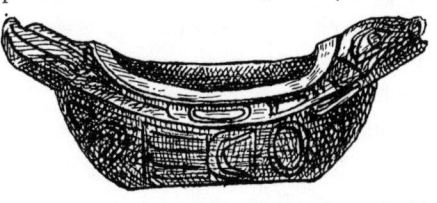

Carved wooden bowl of beautiful shape, and covered with totemic designs.

and singing are indulged in, and the ceremony may at times prolong itself to several days. It need scarcely be added that the receiving of such presents involves a suitable return on some future occasion.

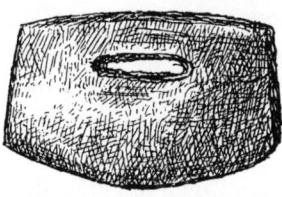

It has been mentioned that dancing takes place at the entertainments I have described, and many of the Indian curiosities which we have brought home are articles of dress or ornament used for ceremonial dancing on these and other festive occasions. We must not think of Indian dancing being such as that to which we are accustomed, in which the whole company takes part; but

Bone bark scraper. This is used for scraping off the inner bark of the cedar, &c., beating it down, preparatory to separating it into fibres for weaving purposes.

it is rather a show performance by the few, the performers being both men and women, whilst others sing or play the drum, shake the rattles, blow the whistles, and thump on the ground with batons to mark the time, and the spectators sit round and look on, and signify applause by grunts and cries of laughter. Niblack classifies three classes of dance—(1) the stately, dignified, and formal; (2) the wild, passionate, and furious; (3) the ludicrous; but, he adds that "the method of dancing them is the same, the movements being slow, or exaggerated, as the case may be. It consists mainly in contortions of the body and hips, with the feet firmly planted and the knees slightly bent. The body is wriggled and swayed from side to side with redoubled animation and fury as the dance advances, but the legs remain bent at about the same angle, and the feet play only a small part in the so-called dancing itself." Masks of all descriptions are worn at these dances—some with eyes that roll and jaws that move, others representing animals with snapping beaks. Then there are ceremonial coats and leggings, and finely worked girdles in beads or in cedar-bark—blankets worked out in totemic designs, and woven in a curious way with the warp of cedar-bark hammered out, and the woof of fine mountain goat's wool (which is found under the animal's outer covering of hair), and batons, wands, head-dresses, ceremonial spears, bows and arrows and I know not what besides.

These articles of apparel are reserved now for these festive occasions, as for ordinary life the Indians have adopted the European costume. There is one ceremonial head-dress used by a chief (represented in the illustration) which I should like you specially to notice. It is carved from hard wood, painted and inlaid with abalone shell, and hanging behind are three lengths of ermine skins; round the top we see remains of a fringe of seal whiskers which surmounted the head-dress, and inside which was placed a quantity of birds' down, which, through the motion of the dancer, would fall like snow around him at his will. This birds' down would also be blown from tubes and scattered otherwise by the dancers, and sometimes it would also be powdered over the paint used on the face and body, thus giving the performer a most startling appearance.

Spoon carved from the horn of a mountain sheep—beautifully executed.

The list of these paraphernalia gives you some idea of the advanced stage to which these Indian races had brought their industrial arts and crafts before the advent of the white man. Their carving, as shown on the totemic columns, funeral and other chests, and on the spoons, bowls, and other household utensils, both on wood, horn, slate, and silver, is marvellous, more especially when the rudeness of their instruments is considered. Their weaving of cloth from cedar-bark and wool has already been alluded to, but their expertness as basket-weavers, canoe-builders, tanners of hides, dyers, and designers, should also be mentioned. These handicrafts are carried on mostly during the winter by men and women alike, and Mr Niblack tells us that the women are quite on an equality with the men in the matters of industrial organisation, that they do a great portion of the trading, and that they take part in the councils. In times of war it was generally an old woman of rank who steered the war canoe.

Unlike the Indians of the interior, the coast Indians are neither good shots nor good hunters as a rule, and seek to obtain their game largely by means of traps, but as fishermen they are unequalled, and we cannot compete, even with our most modern contrivances, with their skill with their crude implements. The Indians parcel out the territory belonging to them, near their villages, in hunting, berrying, and fishing grounds for each household, and their summer camps can be seen near where the salmon run in greatest abundance. Those who have watched the salmon rush up these streams in vast shoals speak of it as a marvellous spectacle: the fish hurling themselves over rocks and waterfalls in their endeavours to surmount all obstacles. The Indians reap their harvest at these times, and never a hook is used. That would be far too slow work—they are either speared or caught in nets, as a rule. But in the catching of all sorts of fish the Indians cannot be surpassed, and we saw all manner of hooks, spears, clubs, floats, nets, and baskets, which they make and use to such good pur-

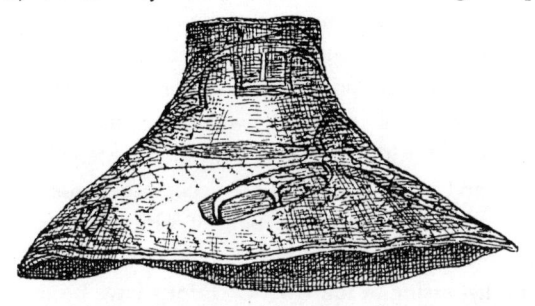

Twined basketry hat. The twining consists of weaving the woof strands round a series of warp strands. Totemic designs are painted on this hat, which is used for dances. Plain hats of this description are used in an ordinary way by both men and women.

pose in catching all kinds of the denizens of sea, and river, and lake. Their fish form a main staple of their food, along with the wild berries that grow in great abundance. Both the fish and berries are dried for the winter's use, and, in former times, if the winter proved long and severe, the Indians were often in want before the fishing began. Now they have learned to cultivate potatoes and other roots to help them through with their winter's supplies. The fish are cut into long flakes, and dried without salt, in the sun, over a slow fire, or in the shade of the dwellings. It is eaten by bits being broken off and dipped into the oil, which is the universal accompaniment of all food. They make a great quantity of oil from bear, deer, goats, seals, porpoises, and all kinds of fish. The fish are allowed partially to putrify, and are then boiled in wooden boxes by means of hot stones dropped in the water. The grease or oil is skimmed from the surface, and is stored in boxes, or in the holy stalks of giant kelp, which are first dried and made pliable with oil. The oil, unfortunately, is often rancid, and this, along with the decomposed roe of fish and putrified salmon heads, both of which are esteemed a great luxury, pervade the Indian dwellings with an odour distressing to the visitor. Efforts have been made to convince them of the insanitary nature of this food, and not without success. The inner bark of spruce, hemlock, and pine, and sea-weed is also used as an article of food, pressed into cakes. One species of sea-weed is used for making a dish called *sopallaly*, of which the Indians are especially fond. It is made by breaking up a piece of the dried sea-weed cake into little bits in a bowl, and adding warm water. It is then beaten with a wooden spoon, and sugar and sometimes berries are added. The mixture froths and foams like the white of an egg, and is consumed with avidity.

There is much else that I would like to tell you about the customs and tradition of this interesting race, but my paper is growing too long, and I fear that I may weary you. But I have not shown you anything of the sad side of the picture—how contact with the whites has demoralised the Indians, how they have intensified the vices of the latter, and how they have introduced new ones—for example, the use of strong liquor, such as rum and a concoction called "*hoochinoo*," a poisonously impure distillation from potatoes. Gambling is a passion with most of the Indians, and we have amongst our collection a specimen of one of the gambling-bags which they carry about, and which are full of small round sticks, which serve them as cards, and on which are found various marks, distinguishing one from the other. The Governments,

Tobacco pouch, with totemic painted designs.

both of British Columbia and Alaska, are doing their best to restrain the drinking and immorality and gambling which have played such havoc amongst the tribes, and the missionaries are carrying on a vigorous work amongst them. These coast tribes are much more susceptible to the influences of Christianity than the tribes of the interior, and the Roman Catholics established successful missions at an early date, which are still flourishing. The Episcopal and other Churches are also at work, and Bishop Sillitoe, of New Westminster, told us that a very marked advance may now be seen in the habits and customs of the people. On one occasion lately he was received after a confirmation ceremony to luncheon by an Indian lady dressed in lavender silk, and a table spread out with preserved fruits and all sorts of delicacies. Advance is also being made in the education and training of the children, and at Yale Lytton, a lovely spot in the mountains, we had the opportunity of seeing a number of bright, attractive-looking little Indian maidens being trained as servants. But I have so little authentic information as to the work of education and missions amongst these Indians that I can only touch on the subject, and hope that I may have sufficiently interested you in these fellow-subjects of ours, whom we have dispossessed, to make you wish to hear more of this side of the subject on some future occasion.

APPENDIX.

THE LATE SIR JOHN A. MACDONALD,
Prime Minister of Canada.

By J. G. COLMER, C.M.G., Secretary at the Office of the High Commissioner for Canada.

IN the July issue of "ONWARD AND UPWARD," the death of the Right Honourable Sir John Alexander Macdonald was briefly referred to, and a promise made that some particulars of his career should be given in a succeeding number. The Editor has been kind enough to afford the opportunity of writing a few words about the deceased statesman; and I will try, in the space at my disposal, to tell my readers what a great and good man he was.

It is not necessary to say very much about the early days of Sir John. He was born in Glasgow in the month of January, 1815, and went to Canada in 1821, with his parents, who were Sutherlandshire people. The party of emigrants settled down near Kingston, on the shores of the beautiful Lake Ontario, and the subject of this little sketch remained identified with the "Limestone City," as it is called, to the day of his death, for, with the exception of one or two intervals, he was its representative, first in the Parliament of Old Canada, and then in that of the Dominion, ever since 1844. Both his father and mother were of good families, but at the time of their settling in Canada were not, to use the ordinary phrase, "well off" from a money point of view. They were, however, good, sensible, people, and it is to their care, and watchfulness, and to their example and training, that Sir John owed most of the remarkable success that he achieved. They contrived to give him as good an education as could be obtained at the time. He acquired a fair average knowledge of classics, and an enormous appetite for reading, but it seems that he especially excelled in mathematics, and in algebra and Euclid he was the "show" boy of the Kingston Grammar School, and the pride of his master. As a lad, he had the peculiar appearance which he retained through life, and one of his biographers describes him in his school days as having "a very intelligent and pleasing face, strange fuzzy-looking hair that curled in a dark mass, and a striking nose." Although full of fun, and blessed with high spirits, he was always a hard worker; and this is the great secret of the advancement and progress of most of our great men. Mr Macdonald was bent on making young John a lawyer, and this object was kept in view in his studies. At the age of fifteen he entered a local "law office," and was called to the bar in 1836, when he reached man's estate.

The next stage was to open a law office on his own account, and as he showed so much ability and diligence in any work he undertook, and, besides was so popular in Kingston and its neighbourhood, he soon acquired the leading practice of the place; and his efforts, although unsuccessful, in the defence of a man named Van Schultz, who, in 1838, tried to create a disturbance in Canada, and entered the country with a number of men from the United States, added greatly to his reputation and gave him a place on the ladder of fame.

Mr John Macdonald, as he was then termed, first entered Parliament in 1844, as I have already stated, and the fact that he became a member of the Administration three years later, shows that he soon assumed a prominent position in the political arena.

From that time, down to the present, his history is that of his adopted country—or, to put it more definitely, of Old Canada up to 1867, and of the Dominion since that year, when several of the

Memorial bust of Sir John Macdonald placed in St Paul's Cathedral, and unveiled by Lord Rosebery, Nov. 1892.

scattered Colonies of British North America agreed to unite under one form of Government. Space will not permit of my discussing, at any length, the events which lead up to the Confederation, but

I may say that the union of Upper and Lower Canada, in 1840, was not found to work easily and smoothly, and there seemed to be no way out of the difficulties that were created until 1864, when the Maritime Provinces were discussing a closer union among themselves at the suggestion of Dr Tupper, now Sir Charles Tupper, the High Commissioner for Canada, in London, whose career is another instance of what ability, energy, and assiduity can accomplish. Well, the long and the short of it was that Canada proposed a much wider union, one which would include all the Colonies; after much negotiation this was brought about, and the new Dominion, with Sir John as the Premier of the first Government, entered upon that era of rapid devlopment, and progress, which has been witnessed in the last twenty-four years, and has attracted attention all over the world. Sir John, as we must now call him (for he received the honour of knighthood in 1867, in recognition of his work), may not have been the originator of the idea of federation, and all the wonderful things that have happened since then may not, as the children say, have come " out of his own head." Still it is generally accepted that much of Canada's success is due to his ability, tact, patience, knowledge of detail, and the remarkable faculty he possessed of conciliating conflicting interests, and smoothing away difficulties. To appreciate the result of the life and labours of Sir John Macdonald, it is necessary to know something of Old Canada fifty years ago, as well as of the great Dominion of to-day. Then British North America consisted of the Maritime Provinces and Canada, the country west of the Lake Huron to the Pacific Coast being under the control of the Hudson Bay Company (the provinces of Manitoba, the North West Territories and British Columbia not being then organised), the great hunting grounds of Indians and trappers, and the home of the buffalo (now extinct), and many other fur-bearing animals. There were only sixteen miles of railway in operation, and all the provinces were as separate and dis-

Appendix.

tinct from each other as are Canada and Australia to-day. What Canada is now the Editor has told us in a delightful manner in this interesting book, descriptive of her journey in 1890, which journey, by the way, would not have been possible but for the efforts of Sir John Macdonald and his colleagues to consolidate the Dominion by the building of the Canadian Pacific Railway, and other public works.

I have nearly come to the end of the space allotted to me, and I cannot write all I should like to say about the many wise measures with which Sir John Macdonald's name is especially identified, besides those dealing with the formation of the Dominion, and the construction of the great railway, which have helped to make the country what it is to-day. But I may add that, apart from the high position he occupied as a statesman, which was recognised in every part of the Empire, he was in his social life a most charming man. No one was more popular in the Dominion among old and young, and no one had more friends. To be in his society was both pleasant and profitable, for he was full of reminiscences and anecdotes, had read everything that is worth reading, and was gifted with a wonderful memory. He was the recipient of many honours from Her Majesty, and his loss has been lamented, not only in the United Kingdom (which found expression in the memorial service in Westminster Abbey), but from one end of Canada to the other. There is very general sympathy with Lady Macdonald in her great grief, and the announcement that the Queen has conferred a peerage upon her, in recognition of her husband's great services to the Empire, has given much satisfaction. It is said that a memorial is to be erected to Sir John's memory in St Paul's Cathedral, and the proposition is such an excellent and appropriate one that it is sure to receive much support. His life affords an example that may well be followed by all young men, both "at home" and in the colonies; for it shows, in the first place, what a man can do for the good of his country, if he throws his heart and soul into his work ; and, secondly, the opportunities for advancement that exist in the Colonies for those who adopt the right methods to earn success. He said of himself, nearly twenty years ago, in the course of a great speech, "There does not exist in Canada a man who has given more of his time, more of his heart, more of his wealth, or more of his intellect and power, such as they may be, for the good of this Dominion of Canada," and those who knew him think that no more appropriate epitaph could be written on the tomb of the lamented statesman than those very words.

On the occasion of unveiling the memorial to the late Right Hon. Sir John Macdonald, in St Paul's Cathedral, on 16th November 1892, the Earl of Rosebery said :—

My Lords, Ladies, and Gentlemen,—It gives me great pleasure to come here to-day to unveil this bust. We are gradually collecting within this cathedral the Lares and the Penates—the household gods—of our commonwealth. Up above there sleep Wellington and Nelson, those lords of war who preserved the Empire ; below here we have the effigies of Dalley and Macdonald, who did so much to preserve it. We have not, indeed, their bodies. They rest more fitly in the regions where they lived and laboured ; but here to-day we consecrate their memory and their example. We know nothing of party politics in Canada on this occasion. We only recognise this—that Sir John Macdonald had grasped the central idea that the British Empire is the greatest secular agency for good now known to mankind ; that that was the secret of his success, and that he determined to die under it, and strove that Canada should live under it. It is a custom, I have heard, in the

German army that when new colours are presented to a regiment the German Emperor first, and then his Princes and chiefs in their order, each drive a nail into the staff. I have sometimes been reminded of this practice in connexion with the banner of our Empire. Elizabeth and her heroes first drove their nails in, and so onward through the expansive 18th century, when our flag flashed everywhere, down to our own times, when we have not quailed or shrunk. Yesterday it wrapped the corpse of Tennyson; to-day we drive one more nail in on behalf of Sir John Macdonald. But this standard, so richly studded, imposes on us—the survivors—a solemn obligation. It would be nothing were it the mere symbol of violence and rapine, or even of conquest. It is what it is because it represents everywhere peace and civilisation and commerce, the negation of narrowness and the gospel of humanity. Let us then to-day, by the shrine of this signal statesman, once more remember our responsibility and renew the resolution that, come what may, we will not flinch or fail under it.

Homeward Bound.

ANNOTATED LIST OF ILLUSTRATIONS

Key
IA: Ishbel, Countess of Aberdeen
NA: National Archives of Canada
HH: Located at Haddo House, Tarves, Aberdeenshire

Page	Caption	Location	Type	Notes
Frontis-piece	Group of Canadian Boys	HH: Canada, 1890–91	Kodak	
Title Page	Unnamed ship	Unidentified	Kodak?	
2	Outward Bound: The *Parisian* dropping down the Mersey	Unidentified	Professional	NA suggests photograph was taken by a British photographer. All NA photographs of this ship were taken in Canadian waters
3	A last peep of 'Ould Ireland'		Sketch (I.A.)	

Annotated List of Illustrations

Page	Caption	Location	Type	Notes
8	The first Iceberg on the Horizon		Sketch (I.A.)	
10	Quebec, from the South Side of the River	Notman Archive Montreal	Professional	Notman copy of a painting by James Weston. A heavily retouched composite, for which Notman was renowned in the 1870s
15	Quebec, from Montmorenci		Sketch (I.A.)	
18	The Falls of Montmorenci	Unidentified	Professional	Almost identical photograph in HH: Canada, 1890–91
21	A Quebec Calèche	HH: Canada, 1890–91	Kodak	
24	Jacques Cartier	HH: Canada, 1890–91	Photograph of engraving	

Annotated List of Illustrations

Page	Caption	Location	Type	Notes
25	Montreal	HH: Canada, 1890–91	Professional	Inaccurate caption. This is the view from Church Hill, Victoria, BC. Original in BC Archives
29	Sir Donald Smith	HH: Canada, 1890–91	Professional	
31	Father Lacombe	Unidentified	Professional	HH: Canada, 1890–91 contains an almost identical photograph, NA has a *carte de visite* by J.E. Livernois of Quebec City, which was probably made at the same sitting as this image was taken. The NA image shows Lacombe standing, looking over his right shoulder, but clothing and accoutrements are the same

Annotated List of Illustrations

Page	Caption	Location	Type	Notes
35	'The First Communion'	Unidentified	Professional	From a Photo of Picture by Jules Breton in the possession of Sir Donald Smith. Lady Aberdeen probably acquired the photograph of this painting through Smith, who would have employed a professional photographer
39	Kingston, Ont.		Sketch (I.A.)	
45	Highfield, Hamilton, Ont.	Unidentified	Professional	HH: Canada, 1890–91 contains other professional photographs of Highfield
47	The Gore, Hamilton, Ont.	Notman Archive	Professional	
49	Lord Haddo. Aged 11	Unidentified	Professional	

Annotated List of Illustrations 255

Page	Caption	Location	Type	Notes
49	Lady Marjorie Gordon. aged 9	Unidentified	Professional	
50	Hon. Dudley and Hon. Archie H. Gordon. Aged 6 and 5	Unidentified	Professional	Family portraits were probably photographed professionally in Britain
51	A Hamilton Yacht	HH: Canada, 1890–91	Sketch	Sketch based on a professional photograph in HH: Canada, 1890–91, probably taken by the same Hamilton photographer as the other Hamilton scenes
55	View on Hamilton Bay	HH: Canada, 1890–91	Professional	
59	The Lads and Lasses who accompanied us to Highfield, and remained in Canada	HH: Canada, 1890–91	Professional	

Annotated List of Illustrations

Page	Caption	Location	Type	Notes
63	University Buildings, Toronto	Unidentified	Sketch	This drawing appears to be based on an unattributed photograph entitled 'Queen's College, Toronto, Ont., c. 1870' in NA (PA-28558)
66	Captain Macmaster	HH: Canada, 1890–91	Professional	
67	Government House, Toronto	Unidentified	Professional	
68	Sir Alexander Campbell, late Lieutenant-Governor of Ontario	Unidentified	Professional	Photograph probably given to Lady Aberdeen by Campbell
73	Falls of Niagara	HH: Canada, 1890–91	Professional	
74	Above Niagara	HH: Canada, 1890–91	Kodak	

Annotated List of Illustrations 257

Page	Caption	Location	Type	Notes
75	View of Ottawa	Notman Archive	Professional	
76	Lord Stanley	HH: Canada, 1890–91	Professional	
77	Lady Stanley	HH: Canada, 1890–91	Professional	
79	Sir John Abbott, Prime Minister of Canada	HH: Canada, 1890–91	Professional	Inaccurate caption. This is a photograph of Sir John Carling, Minister of Agriculture
80	A pair of Aceedian or San-whet Owls	Unidentified	Professional	Should read 'Saw-whet Owls'
81	Canadian Dick and Bill at Dollis Hill, Willesden	HH: Canada, 1890–91	Professional	Carbon printed
84	The View from the Terrace outside Parliament Buildings, Ottawa	Unidentified	Professional	

Annotated List of Illustrations

Page	Caption	Location	Type	Notes
87	Rideau Hall, Ottawa, the residence of the Governor-General	HH: Canada, 1890–91	Professional	
89	The Toboggan-Slide at Rideau Hall	HH: Canada, 1890–91	Professional	
90	Westward!	Unidentified	Kodak	HH: Canada, 1890–91 contains almost identical photographs
92	All Aboard!	Unidentified	Kodak	HH: Canada, 1890–91 contains almost identical photograph
93	The Car in which we travelled West	HH: Canada, 1890–91	Kodak	
95	John Barber, our Car-Porter		Sketch, probably based on photograph	

Annotated List of Illustrations

Page	Caption	Location	Type	Notes
96	A Young Settlement	Unidentified	Kodak	
98	Mr O'Brien (who christened the Lake of Killarney) and his wife talking to Lord Aberdeen	HH: Canada, 1890–91	Kodak	
99	All that is left of the buffalo	HH: Canada, 1890–91	Kodak	Very poor quality in original
101	How a journey from Winnipeg for Ottawa was accomplished in days gone by	Unidentified	Professional	This may have been intended as a joke. While there may have been a dog-team which went from Fort Garry to Ottawa, it was not the regular procedure implied in the caption. NA has a photograph of the sledge and possibly even the same dog-team, but not

260 Annotated List of Illustrations

Page	Caption	Location	Type	Notes
				this particular shot. The word 'Norway' is written on the side of the sledge, which might indicate it came from Norway House, 460 km north of Winnipeg, hub of the Hudson Bay Company's fur trade and supply lines
104	Manitou, Manitoba	HH: Canada, 1890–91	Kodak	
106	Greetings from a group of Manitobans at Manitoba	HH: Canada, 1890–91	Kodak	
109	Mr and Mrs Peter Graham's Cottage	HH: Canada, 1890–91	Professional	
110	Mr and Mrs John Campbell's house	HH: Canada, 1890–91	Kodak	

Annotated List of Illustrations 261

Page	Caption	Location	Type	Notes
111	The Darough family at Glenfern	HH: Canada, 1890–91	Sketch from professional photograph	
115	Scene of Accident, from a sketch made by Lady Aberdeen same night		Sketch (I.A.)	
116	Our Engine as photographed by the Kadok [sic] the morning after the accident	Unidentified	Kodak	
117	Off again!	Unidentified	Kodak	
122	A regiment of workers on the Prairie	Unidentified	Sketch	
124	One of Sir John Lister-Kaye's big farms in Alberta	Unidentified	Kodak	

Annotated List of Illustrations

Page	Caption	Location	Type	Notes
125	Passing a car-full of emigrants – 'Take our pictures'	Unidentified	Kodak	
126	Map showing region of summer droughts in North America			
127	A horse ranch near Calgary	Unidentified	Kodak	
132	Approaching the Rockies	HH: Canada, 1890–91	Kodak	
133	'The Three Sisters'	Unidentified	Sketch from professional photograph	HH: Canada, 1890–91 contains almost identical photograph
135	From the window of the Banff Hotel	HH: Canada, 1890–91	Kodak	

Annotated List of Illustrations 263

Page	Caption	Location	Type	Notes
136	Cascade Mountain, Banff	Unidentified	Sketch from professional photograph	Inaccurate caption. This is Mount Rundle, not Cascade Mountain. HH: Canada, 1890–91 contains almost identical photograph
139	The Van Horne Range – sketched from Field by Lady Aberdeen		Sketch (I.A.)	
140	A Trestle Bridge	HH: Canada, 1890–91	Professional	View down Fraser River, BC. Original photograph in Notman Archive, one of a set of about 81 8x10's (all 1885) attributed to J.W. Heckman
142	Vancouver	HH: Canada, 1890–91	Professional	Bailey & Co. Vancouver Public Library

Annotated List of Illustrations

Page	Caption	Location	Type	Notes
143	The late Mr G.G. MacKay	Unidentified	Professional	Similar photograph located in BC Archives
146	His Honour the Lieut.-Governor of British Columbia	BC Archives	Professional	
147	Admiral Hotham	Unidentified	Professional	Similar photograph located in BC Archives
148	H.M.S. 'Warspite'	Unidentified	Professional	Similar photograph located in BC Archives
151	Lord Aberdeen and Professor H. Drummond in the Railway Car	HH: Canada, 1890–91	Kodak	
157	The first passenger train on the Shushwap [sic] and Okanagan Line halting at Enderby	HH: Canada, 1890–91	Kodak	Poor quality in original

Annotated List of Illustrations 265

Page	Caption	Location	Type	Notes
159	Mr Lequime's little steamer which took us up the Lake to Guisachan	HH: Canada, 1890–91	Professional	Caption in album reads: 'Mr *Gunn's* little steam-boat in which we were conveyed by moonlight from Vernon to Guisachan'
160	Transferring the baggage from the train to the steamer	HH: Canada, 1890–91	Kodak	Very poor quality in original
162	Entrance Gate to Guisachan Farm	HH: Canada, 1890–91	Kodak	Poor quality in original
163	In the woods of Guisachan, B.C.	HH: Canada, 1890–91	Kodak	Very poor quality in original
165	View from the front-door of Guisachan. From a sketch by Lady Aberdeen		Sketch (I.A.)	
166	Guisachan, B.C.	HH: Canada, 1890–91	Kodak	

Annotated List of Illustrations

Page	Caption	Location	Type	Notes
170	Going out for a bear hunt	HH: Canada, 1890–91	Kodak	
171	Watching the game-bag	HH: Canada, 1890–91	Kodak	
172	'Foo,' our Chinese cook	HH: Canada, 1890–91	Kodak	
173	Willy, the Indian boy, with his white pony	HH: Canada, 1890–91	Kodak	
174	Residence No. 1. Present owner emerging from inspection	HH: Kodak snaps by IA	Kodak	
175	Residence No. 2	HH: Kodak snaps by IA	Kodak	
176	Residence No. 3	HH: Kodak snaps by IA	Kodak	

Annotated List of Illustrations

Page	Caption	Location	Type	Notes
177	Residence No. 4	HH: Kodak snaps by IA	Kodak	
179	The Guisachan staff	HH: Kodak snaps by IA	Kodak	
180	Starting for a drive with 'Charlie' and 'Pinto'	HH: Kodak snaps by IA	Kodak	
181	Mr Smith exhibiting the wild Indian pony	HH: Kodak snaps by IA	Kodak	Poor quality in original. In original photography, pony is looking away from camera; in the image reproduced in the book, it is facing camera
183	Coutts on 'Aleck' – 'Spot' in attendance	HH: Kodak snaps by IA	Kodak	
187	Planting Scotch Firs from Guisachan, Invernessshire, at Guisachan, B.C.	HH: Kodak snaps by IA	Kodak	Poor quality in original

Annotated List of Illustrations

Page	Caption	Location	Type	Notes
191	S.S. 'Penticton' waiting to bear us away	HH: Kodak snaps by IA	Kodak	Poor quality in original
193	Good-bye!	HH: Kodak snaps by IA	Kodak	
199	Going to work at Coldstream Ranch	HH: Canada, 1890–91	Professional	
201	The S.S. 'Empress of India' steaming out of Vancouver, en route to Japan	HH: Canada, 1890–91	Kodak	Image reproduced in book was taken immediately after image reproduced in album
209	Deligalugaseitsa and Sepistopota, Sarcee Indians	HH: Canada, 1890–91	Professional	Boorne & May. Notman Archive
213	'Crowfoot,' Chief of the Blackfeet	Notman Archive	Professional	Original by Alexander Ross, Calgary, late 1880s. Caption in book reads

Annotated List of Illustrations 269

Page	Caption	Location	Type	Notes
				Blackfeet, whereas the correct name is Blackfoot
214	A collection of clubs and whips, weighted with stones and metals, which the Indians throw with marvellous dexterity		Sketch (Mr J. Grant)	
215	A feather head-dress for ceremonial and war dances. It is worn down the back of the head		Sketch (Mr J. Grant)	Neither these sketches, nor those done by Lady Aberdeen, are available in the original. All reproductions have been made from *Through Canada with a Kodak* (Edin., 1893)
216	Belt of feathers worn in time of war and at ceremonial dances		Sketch (Mr J. Grant)	

Annotated List of Illustrations

Page	Caption	Location	Type	Notes
217	A papoose swathed on its cradle-board		Sketch (Mr J. Grant)	
219	Making a 'brave' at the sun-dance	Notman Archive	Sketch from photograph	Photograph by Boorne & May
221	An Indian lodge or wigwam	Notman Archive	Sketch from photograph	Photograph by Boorne & May
224	Eastern part of Kasa-an Village, Prince of Wales Island, Alaska. (From 'The Coast Indians of Alaska and British Columbia' by Niblack)		Sketch from book	
225	Model of totem column erected outside an Indian house		Sketch (Mr J. Grant)	
226	Chief's ceremonial head-dress. Explained on p. 237		Sketch (Mr J. Grant)	

Annotated List of Illustrations

Page	Caption	Location	Type	Notes
227	Mask used for ceremonial purposes and formerly for war. The jaws move by pulling a string. The face is painted with totemic designs		Sketch (Mr J. Grant)	
228	Rattle used in ceremonial dances, and also by the Shaman or medicine-man. Carved with totemic designs		Sketch (Mr J. Grant)	
229	Medicine-man's apron. Totem of eagle worked in red cloth, and below three rows of puffin beaks to rattle as wearer moves		Sketch (Mr J. Grant)	
231	Chief's coat, made of beautifully tanned buck-		Sketch (Mr J. Grant)	

Page	Caption	Location	Type	Notes
	skin and edged with velvet and fur. These coats are often covered over with totemic designs			
232	Fringed leggings to wear with chief's coat. Each legging used separately		Sketch (Mr J. Grant)	
233	Chief's bead-embroidered girdle, gambling bag, dagger sheath, and pistol pouch. Used for ceremonial occasions		Sketch (Mr J. Grant)	
234	Bow and arrows and buckskin actually used by an old chief		Sketch (Mr J. Grant)	
235	Carved wooden bowl of beautiful shape, and		Sketch (Mr J. Grant)	

Page	Caption	Location	Type	Notes
	covered with totemic designs			
235	Bone bark scraper. This is used for scraping off the inner bark of the cedar, etc., beating it down, preparatory to separating it into fibres for weaving purposes		Sketch (Mr J. Grant)	
237	Spoon carved from the horn of a mountain sheep – beautifully executed		Sketch (Mr J. Grant)	
239	Twined basketry hat		Sketch (Mr J. Grant)	
241	Tobacco pouch, with totemic painted designs		Sketch (Mr J. Grant)	

Page	Caption	Location	Type	Notes
245	Memorial bust of Sir John Macdonald placed in St Paul's Cathedral and unveiled by Lord Rosebery, Nov. 1892	Unidentified	Professional	
249	Homeward Bound	Unidentified	Kodak	Same ship as on title page

INDEX

Abbott, Sir John, xxxi, lxi, 78
Aberdeen, Countess of: advice to emigrants, xxxvii, xxxix, 12, 122–4, 147, 150, 178, 194–5, 247–8; advocates emigration, xxi–xxii, xxxviii, xliii, xlix, liv, lvii, lxiv, lxxiii, 5–6, 28, 39, 58–60; charity work, xvii–xviii, xix–xxii, 103; childhood, xvii; impressions of Indians, lxix–lxxii, 202–42; involved in railway accident, lv, 113–19; journal, xxii, xxiii, xxxv, lvi–lvii, lviii, lxi, 28, 107; Liberalism, xviii–xix, xxii, lxii; reflections on travel, 57, 94, 149; travels by CPR, 91–7, 113–34; travel writings, xv–xvi, xxiii, xxxiii–xxxv, xl, lxxiii–lxxv; use of Kodak, xxvi–xxviii, lv, lxi, 4, 14, 78, 97, 109, 118, 137, 182, 190; voyage to Canada, xxxvi–xxxix, 1–9
Aberdeen, Earl of, xviii, xix, xxxix, lvii, lxi, 4, 23, 40, 137, 155, 158; BC properties, xlix, lxii–lxv, 123, 161, 166, 175–6, 185, 192–6; and Indians, lxxi, 231–2; Governor General of Canada, xxii, xxx, xlviii, lxxiv; in Ontario, 43–4, 56, 60, 64, 69, 77, 79, 81
Aberdeen, Scotland, xxi
Aberdeen Association, li, lx, 102–3
Aberdeen Ladies' Union, xxi–xxii, xxxviii–xxxix
Aberdeenshire, xviii–xix, xlvii, lvi, 123, 137
Abraham, Plains of, xl
Alaska, 225, 241
Albert, Prince Consort, xxiv

Index

Alberta, lvi, 126–7, 182, 216
Allan, George, xlvii, 69
America. *See* United States
Australia, xxiii, xliv, lviii, 1, 149

Baden Powell, Sir George, 103
Banff, xxviii, xxxi, lvii, lx, lxii, 134–7, 154, 186
Banff Springs Hotel, lvii, 134–5
Barber, John, 94
Barclay, James, xlii, 30, 33
Barnardo, Dr Thomas, xxxviii
Barron (Lady Aberdeen's maid), xxxvii, 174–5
bear-hunting, lxiii, 86, 169–72
Bird, Robert Montgomery, lxviii
Blackfoot Indians, lxxii, 207, 208, 210–11
Blake, Edward, xlvii, 69
Boorne and May, xxviii, xxix–xxx, lxx, 268, 270
Bow River, 134
British Association, 205
British Columbia, xxxi, xxxv, lii, 141–9, 154–8, 198–200, 246; advice to emigrants, 194–5; Archives, xxx, xxxi, 253, 263, 264; Indians, lxxi, 205, 223–42; Okanagan properties, xlix, lvi, lxii–lxvi, 123, 153, 158–9
Brock, General, xlv, 216–17
buffalo, 98, 203, 206, 208, 246

Calgary, xxx, xxxiv, lvi, 128, 215, 220, 268
California, 161
Campbell, Sir Alexander, xlvi–xlvii, 16, 67–9
Campbell, Marjorie, 69
Canada: agricultural fairs, xxxiii, xlvi, 60, 61–7, 69, 72, 80–1,

Index

112, 155, 158–9, 161–4; Chinese in, lxiii, 141, 146–7, 168, 174, 175–8, 200–2; farming, 20, 82–3, 108–12, 122–6; French, xl–xli, 9, 11–12, 16–17, 19–21, 37; fruit growing, lx, lxiv–lxv, 72, 161, 182; guidebooks and travelogues, xiii–xvi, xxxiii–xxxv, xlv–xlvi, lxxiii–lxxv, 94; immigration to, xiii–xiv, xxii, xxxvii–xxxix, xlviii, xlix, l–lvi, lxiv, 5, 7, 11–13, 28, 39, 58–60, 96, 103–12, 123–4, 137, 147, 184, 194–5; National Archives, xxvii–xxviii, xxxv, 251, 253, 256; Presbyterian Church, 185–6; Scots in, xlvii, lii–lv, lvii, lxiii, 78, 100, 103–12, 137–40, 142, 156; voyage to, xxxvi–xxxix, 1–9; wages in, 12, 147, 182

Canadian Mounted Police, 127, 137

Canadian Pacific Railway, xlvii, li, lvii, 30, 144, 200, 212, 134; Aberdeens travel on, xlviii–xlix, lx–lxi, lxii, 91–7, 113–41, 154–8; accident on, lv, 113–19; construction of, xlii, 140–1, 247

Carling, Sir John, xxxi, xlvii, 82

carte de visite, xxv, xxviii

Carter, Paul, xxxiii, xxxv

Cartier, Jacques, xl, xli, 14, 24

Cascade Mountain, xxviii, xxxi

Chambers' Journal, lxix

Champlain, Samuel de, xl, 16

Chicago World Fair, lxvi, 223

Chinese. *See* Canada, Chinese in

City of Paris, lxvi

Cobourg, xliii

Coldstream Ranch, lxiii–lxv, 193–4, 196, 197–8

Colmer, J.G., 243

Columbia River, 131

Conckling, Frank, 182

Cooper, James Fenimore, lxviii
Corsican, xlii–xliii, 37–8, 40–1
Côteau, xlii, 37
Crofters' War, liii
Crowfoot, Chief of the Blackfoot, lxxii, 212–15
Cruso, Mr (steamboat agent), xliii, 41
curling, 88–90

Dakota, xxiii, xlix, 107, 178, 182
Darough family, 111–12
domestic servants, xix, xx, xxi, lxxiii, lxxv, 12–13, 147
Drummond, Henry, lvii–lix, lx–lxi, 149
Dundas, 72

Eastman, George, xxv–xxvii
Edinburgh, Scotland, xv, xvi
emigrants, xxxvi, xxxvii, xlviii, 4–5, 11–12; difficulties of, l–lii, 96–7, 102–3; female, xxxvii–xxxviii, xliii, 5–6, 13, 28, 39; on prairies, l–lv, 96–7, 102–12, 122–3, 124; religious facilities for, 33, 185–6; Scandinavian, 6–7, 112; Scottish, xlvii, lii–lv, lvi, lvii, 78, 103–12, 123, 137–8, 142, 156
emigration, xiii, xv, xxxii, lxxiii, 58–60, 150; agents, xiv, xxiv, 1; female, xvi–xvii, xxi–xxii, xxxiv, xxxviii, xxxix, xli, lix, lxxiii, 12–13, 39, 147, 178; juvenile, xxxvii–xxxviii, xlviii–xlix; to BC, lxii–lxiii, lxiv, lxv, 178, 184, 194–5
Empress of India, 198–200
Enderby, 156
Erie Canal, xlv
Esquimault, 148

Foo (Chinese cook), 168, 174, 175–6
Fraser Valley, lx

Index

French Canada, xl–xli, 9, 11–12, 16–17, 19–21, 37

gentlemen emigrants, lxii–lxiii
Gladstone, William Ewart, xviii–xix, xxii, lxii
Gordon, George (Lord Haddo), xlviii, 43–4
Gordon, Marjorie (Lady Pentland), liii, lxi, 50, 155, 164, 174, 189
Government Experimental Farm (Ottawa), 82–3, 100
Grant, Sir James, 78
guidebooks. *See* travelogues
Guisachan, lx, lxii–lxv, 153, 162–96, 197, 198

Haddo, Scotland, xviii–xx, lxii, 156, 223; photographic collection, xxvii, xxviii–xxix, xxx, lxx
Haddo House Association. *See* Onward and Upward Association
Hamilton, xxvii, xli, xliv–xlv, lx, 42–57, 72
Harper, Captain (RCMP), 137
Highfield, xliv–xlv, xlviii, lx, 42–50, 58–9
Home Children, xxxvii–xxxviii, xlviii–xliv, 5–6, 13
Home for Female Emigrants (Montreal), xxxix, xli, 28
homesteading, l–lvi
Horseshoe Ranch (Dakota), xlix
Hotham, Admiral, 148, 149
Hudson's Bay Company, xlii, lvi, 28, 74, 128, 129–30, 246

immigration. *See* Canada, immigration to; emigration
imperialism, xiv, xl, lvii, lxxi–lxxiii, lxxv, 19, 52–3, 248
India, xxiii, 1
Indians, xxxv, xlii, lxvi–lxxiii, 16, 24–6, 36, 97, 128–30, 141, 202–42; missions to, xlii, 30–3, 130, 184, 204, 241–2; of

BC, 223–42; plight of, lxix–lxx, lxxi–lxii, 202–4, 241; religion and customs of, 205–11, 218–22, 226–40
International Council of Women, xviii
Ireland, xvii, 3–4
Irish, 39, 108, 142; Home Rule, xxii

Jackfish Bay, 97
Japan, lviii, 149
Johnson, Dr Samuel, xxxii, lxxv
Joyce, Ellen, 13

Kelowna, lxii
Kicking Horse Pass, 131
Killarney, Manitoba, xxviii, xxxv, lii–lv, 107
Kingston, xliii, 39–40, 243, 244
Kodak: invention of, xxv–xxvi; use of, xxvi–xxvii, liv, lv, lxi, 4, 6, 14, 78, 97, 109–10, 118, 137, 182, 190

Labrador, xlii, 9, 28
Lachine Rapids, xliii, 27, 36–7
Lacombe, Albert, xlii, 30–2
Lake of the Woods, 97
land developers, xiv. *See also* MacKay, George
lantern slides, xxiv
Laud, Robert, 54
Laurier, Sir Wilfrid, xiii
Lister-Kaye, Sir John, lvi, 123, 137
Liverpool, England, xxxvi, lx, lxvi, 7
Liverpool Home for the Orphan Children of Seamen, 7
London, England, xv, xvii, xx, xxvi, 27, 62, 66, 82, 182, 246
London, Ontario, xlvi, 61–2, 69

Long Lake, 198
Lothian, Lord, liii, 104, 106
lumber industry, 83-8, 105

Macdonald, Lady Agnes, lxii, 119, 247
Macdonald, Sir John A., xxxv, xlvii, lxi, lxvi, 77, 78; obituary, 243-9
Macdougall family (Guisachan), 181-2
MacKay, George G., lix-lx, lxiii, lxiv, 144, 161, 192, 194, 195
Mackie, Dr (Kingston clergyman), xliii
Macpherson, Annie, xxxviii, xlviii-xlix, 5
Maissonneuve, Sieur de, xli, 26
Manitoba, xlvii, l-lvi, 20, 97, 100-26, 246
Mara Lake, 156
Maritime Provinces, 246
Marjoribanks, Archibald, xxiii
Marjoribanks, Coutts, xxiii, xlix, lx, 98, 107, 112; in Okanagan Valley, lix, lxii, lxiii, 162, 166-7, 195
Marjoribanks, Edward, xviii
Medicine Hat, lx, 127
Mercier, Honoré, xli
Methlick, xx, lvi, 123
Métis, xlii
Montcalm, Marquis de, xl, 16, 17
Montmorenci Falls, 17
Montreal, xxix-xxx, xxxix, xl, xli-xlii, lxi, 23-37, 76
Moody, Dwight, lxi
Mount Rundle, xxviii, xxxi
Mowat, Oliver, xlvii, 69

National Archives of Canada, xxvii-xxviii, xxxv

Native People. *See* Indians
Nelson, Hugh, lviii–lix, 147–8
Newfoundland, 8, 9
New Westminster, 242
New York, lix, lx, lxi, lxvi
New Zealand, xxiii, 1
Niagara Falls, xlv–xlvi, lxxiv, 17, 71
Niagara-on-the-Lake, xxxviii
Northwest (North-West) Territories, xlii, lii, lvi, 127, 161, 191, 246
Notman, William, xxix–xxx, 252, 254, 263, 268, 270

Okanagan Lake, 164, 170, 172, 196
Okanagan Mission, 184
Okanagan Valley, lx, lxiii–lxv, lxxii, 154, 158–98; fruit farming, lxiv–lxv, 159–61, 184, 190–7
Ontario, xlvi–xlvii, 52, 72, 111, 182; Lake, xliii, 40–2, 243
Onward and Upward Associates, li, lvi, 113, 123
Onward and Upward Association, xx, 4, 28, 56, 123
Onward and Upward magazine, xv, xx–xxi, li, lxi, 50, 65, 78, 81, 196, 243
Oppenheimer, David, 142
Orphan Homes of Scotland, xxxviii
Ottawa, xliv, xlvii–xlviii, lx, lxi, 72–90; Government Experimental Farm, 82–3; sawmills, 83–5

Parisian, xxxvi–xxxix, 1–9, 14, 16, 23
Pelican Lake, 110
Pendozy (Pandosy), Father Charles, 184
photographs, xxiii–xxxi; defects in, xxviii–xxix, xxx–xxxi, 78, 182, 196. *See also* Kodak

Index

Plains of Abraham, xl, 16
Postill family (Guisachan), 186, 188
prairies, xlvii, l–lvi, lxi, 107–12, 119–23, 131
Prince of Wales Island, 226

Quarrier, William, xxxviii–xxxix
Quebec, province of, 17–21
Quebec City, xxxix–xli, 11–17, 21–2

railway companies, xiv, lxxii. *See also* Canadian Pacific Railway
Regina, 127
Rideau Hall, xlvii–xlviii, 88
Ritchie, Captain, xxxvi, xxxix, 23
Rocky Mountains, xlviii, lvi, lxxiv, 94, 128, 131–5, 205, 206, 207
Roman Catholicism, xl
romanticism, xiv, xl, xlv–xlvi
Rosebery, Earl of, xviii, 248
Ross, Alexander, 268
Rye, Maria, xxxviii, xxxix, 5–6, 13

St Lawrence River, xxxix, 9, 14, 36, 38
St Paul's Cathedral, 247, 248
Saltcoats, lii, liii, lv
Salvation Army, xxxvi
Sanford, William, xliv
San Francisco, lviii
Scotland, xviii–xx, xxix, xxxviii, 138; Highlands, lii–lv, lix, 103–12. *See also* Canada, Scots in; emigrants, Scottish
Selkirk Mountains, 131

Shaughnessy, Thomas, xlii, 30
Shuswap Lake, 155
Sicamous, lxii, 154, 155
Sinclair, John (Lord Pentland), lvii–lviii
Smith, Mr (Guisachan assistant-manager), 166–7, 174
Smith, Annie, xliii, 39
Smith, Sir Donald, xlii, xlviii, xlix, 28–30, 33–4, 97–8, 100
Smithsonian Institute, 223
Spallumcheen River, 156
Stanley, Lord, xliv, 13
Stead, W.T., xx
stereoscopes, xxiv

Tarland, Scotland, 137
Tarves, Scotland, xix
Texas, xxiii, 107
Thompson, Sir John, 78
Thousand Islands, xliii, 38
Three Sisters Mountain, xxviii, 131
Thunder Bay, 97
tobogganing, 88
Topley, William James, xxx
Toronto, xxvii, xxxiii–xxxiv, 42, 61–70, 76; Autumn Fair, xxxiii, xlvi, 61–7
travelogues, xiii–xvi, xxiii, xxxi–xxxv, xl–xli, xlv–xlvi, lxvi, lxxiii–lxxv; deceptiveness of, 94; Indians represented in, lxvi–lxix
Trutch, Sir Joseph, lix, 147
Tupper, Sir Charles, 246
Turner (Lord Aberdeen's servant), xxxvii, 175

Umbria, lx
United British Women's Emigration Society, 13
United Empire Loyalists, 52–4
United States, xiii, xxiii, xxvi, lxi, lxvi, 52, 182, 244

Vancouver, lviii, lix–lx, lxvi, 141–5, 198, 223
Vernon, lxii, 155, 158, 164, 186, 196, 197; jam factory in, lxiv, 192–3
Vernon, Forbes, lxiii, 158
Victoria, Queen, xxiv, 247
Victoria (BC), xxxi, lviii–lix, 141, 145–6, 223
Victorian Order of Nurses, xviii

White, W.H. & Co., xv–xvi
Will, John, lvi, 123
Wilson, Rev. E., 205
Windsor Hotel (Montreal), xli, 23
Winnipeg, xlix–l, li, lx, 97–103, 113, 114, 119
Wolfe, General James, xl, 16–17
Women's Liberal Federation, xvii
Women's National Health Association of Ireland, xvii
Women's Protective Immigration Society (Quebec City), xxxix, 12

Yale Lytton, 242
Yorkshire, 182